Erotic
&
Romantic Poetry

Erotic & Romantic Poetry

Lyrical Poet

Copyright © 2011 by Lyrical Poet.

ISBN: Softcover   978-1-4568-6317-3

All rights reserved. No part of this book may be reproduced or transmitted in any form or by any means, electronic or mechanical, including photocopying, recording, or by any information storage and retrieval system, without permission in writing from the copyright owner.

This book was printed in the United States of America.

To order additional copies of this book, contact:
Xlibris Corporation
1-888-795-4274
www.Xlibris.com
Orders@Xlibris.com
93515

Dedication

I would like to thank all my Facebook fans and friends who made the dream of writing this book a reality by their constant quest for a book featuring all the 4 poets herein.

I would also like to thank Boston M, jay jahs, Emmanuel, Peter, and Dj AZ, for their support and encouragement while undertaking this project.

Book Cover Art by Darryl Blanchard Sr.

Contents

LYRICAL POET

Fan_damental Bliss 13
You're still the one 16
Whore-rizon 18
Nobody cares! 20
"Fuck it!" 22
Confession 24
Lick u all night 25
Kitty Kat 27
Eyee-ing 29
Beauty lies in the eyes of the beer-holder 30
I don't give a phuck 32
Dicktation 34
Kitchen flavor 36
Please don't stop!!! 38
Sex 41
Allergic to gals 43
Garlgaliciouse 44
Take care 45
She already knows 46
Freak or sleek? 48
Can tease can't please 49
Sex is sweet 51
Am not in the mood 54
Let kids be kids 56
Pussydicktion 58
Pussy talk 59
Sexual anthem 61
I love the way you lie 62
I fucked them all 63

POEMS BY DAWN BLANCHARD DEEP RIVERS

Addiction...69
Is It Me I See..70
Well Put Together..72
Gotta have it..73
Connections...74
Take N Time..75
Dreaming, Don't Wake Me 76
Power...77
Hungry 79
Let's Play 81
Quickie..83
Morning Love 84
Hypnotic..85
Desire 86
Let's talk..87
Taboo...88
My breast 89
Inner sanctity...90
Drive 91
Listen...92
Damn!!..93
Clouds 94
Relaxing 95
Second chance...96
Still..97

POEMS BY BROCKELLE NELSON

About me...101
Try Us and See..102
Spoken Words 104
Spin Cycle...106
Real Life Dick Miracle 107
Mathematical Sex Part 2 109
A Love Story To Dick...111
Relive The Conquest!..112
Conversational Mind Orgasms............................114

Do It Myself	116
Greatest Philosophical Sex	118
Mind Fuck Me 1	120
Meow . . . Miss Kitty	123
Mind Fuck Me II	125
He Has To Push	127
Boop . . . Ey Qunicy	129
Boop . . . Q Train	132
Climax, Where Are You?	134
69x3=Mathematical Sex	136
He Shot Me-Deep Throat Tale	138
Yes, I suck dick!	140
PU-NA-NY (caramel w a side of hellafied)	143
Phone Sex Hangover	147
My pen is my mechanical dick (no comparison)	150
7 Minutes to sunrise: a tryst with a celebrity	152
WOW Factor	155
Downtown (Bite and Chew)	157

POEMS BY KLAVON CLAIRMONT

Biography:	163
Write to me my lyrical	165
Drips Drips	167
Bring me to life	169
Roses Part One	171
Petals of Passion	173
A Breath of Fresh Air	175
The Effect of A Kiss That's Not On Your Lips	177
Bathroom Intimacies	179
Friend or Foe	182
Gone forever	185
Afraid of Commitment	188
Drink Me	190
You are in my dreams.	191
Close your eyes and let me invade your mind	193
Let Me Be Your Lover	195
Why I Can't Make Love To You	196
Your Weakness	198

The Signature	199
What's In a Kiss	201
Latin Lust	203
If I Could Love You	204
If You Could See Yourself Through My Eyes	206
The Profile Picture	208
How I Love Your Finger	210
The Best I Ever Had	212

Lyrical poet

About the author:
An erotic junkie

Favorite quote
"Stupidity is a privilege,
Available to all,
Affordable to fools
But expensive to the wise"

Real name-Patrick kokello, but known to many by his
Author/stage name, (Lyrical poet)
Nationality- Kenyan,
Published his first book "Thinking loud
Allowed "in 2008
His next project is poetry book collaboration with Dawn Blanchard, titled "back n forth"
Also in writing are two erotic novels namely
1) "Fuckation"_ when does your vacation end up being a fuckation.
2) Whore_rizon.

Contact:
Email. *lyricalpoet@live.com*
http://www. Lyricalerotics.com

Fan_damental Bliss

Educated guess underneath her skirt
Filled with grin she knows am a flirt

Playa playa, she attracted to my style
The smooth operator that makes her smile

Glasses blinking, "tell me it's real"
I love ur writing, u the fucking deal

Thanx for the love but I don't do these
"Oh common poet, so u don't like these?"

Wonderful tts overflowing from her chest
"Naughty poet u allowed to taste"

Temptations arise, I try to resist
But she guides my hands to pay them a visit

Succulent plums, my hands are full
These Pamela Andersons are hard to resist.

"Am your number one fan, I need your treat"
Ego stroked, I can't retreat

Life is short no time to plot
Come what may let me give it a shot

Edging closer for a simple kiss
Lips merge without a miss

Adam n eve couldn't have been wrong
Passions ignited the night is long

Chests heave in heavy hiss
Her hands on my dick," I want this"

A closet freak n mistress in her craft,
She holds n gently strokes my shaft,

Placing her tongue for a gentle glide,
Along my tender sensitive underside,

She looks up at me with her sexy eyes,
As her head moon walks between my thighs

Gently massaging my manhood's tip,
With her soft tongue and lower lip

My dick rock solid in a state of bliss
She can read my mind it's time to please

She abandons the blow-job she gives so free
 In readiness for a lusting fucking spree

Her thong takes a holiday on my bedroom door nail
 Her kitty set to host my dick in style

Right hand sliding up her thigh
Her temperature rises to an all time high

Pussy lips parted like a recipe book
Middle finger inserted with a twisted hook

Pulling upwards she suddenly moans
G-spot provoked, pussy throbs

Sweet talking her pussy seductive wet
She knows tonight it will be my favorite pet

The lyrical effect has gotten her high
So is time to rumble in her diamond thighs

Eyes interlock mid air with thirst
Her fingernails burrow my butt with lust

"Push it deeper make me concede,
that ur 8 inches dick there's nothing to impede"

Hard and faster she takes it all
Body trembling she starts to call

"Please cum for me I can't take it anymore
Please cum for me my pussy is soar"

Faster n faster I increase the speed
And finally eject to her call to heed

She moans and squirts to the lyrical effect
Juices mingling we all connect

Bodies dripping amassed in sweat
Muscles trembling from the joyful beat.

Exhausted from hours of FAN-damental bliss
We lay in bed in perfect bliss
The fan poet experience forever to remember

You're still the one

You're still the one that makes feel at home
The one that makes home a fun place to come

You're still the one that gives me solace
The one in whose heart I call my place

You're still the one that makes me calm
The one who wipes my tears with her palm

You're still the one that makes me smile
The one who makes me happy from a mile

You're still the one who has thrown me in frenzy
The one that I love when I miss I go crazy

You're still the one in whose eyes I find satisfaction
The better half of my heart that completes the equation

You're still the one in whose heart I see a finesse
The one angel in whom I find my happiness

You're still the one in whose soul I find a mate
The one in whose love I bind my fate

You're still the one in whom I seek a favor
The one that has my heart endeared to her flavor

You're still the one in whom I have bestowed my trust
The one princess charming that i truly love n not lust

You're still the one that I have banked my everything on
The one whose inner beauty and wonderful attributes turn me on

The one that I seek to feed my clamor
The one to give my all love glory n glamour
The one in whose heart I find my joy
The one that makes my heart melt like alloy
  You're my one and only of a kind.

Whore-rizon

Driving down Miami Beach
I met this Trina type baddest bitch

Toppling on Jimmy Chou six inch heels
With a macjacob's bag emblazoned in steel

She had Alicia keys braids and a beautiful face,
Wearing a tight miniskirt of leather and lace

It didn't take more than just a glance,
To realize in her skirt I wanted a chance

So i walked up fast to catch with her pace
Enough for a glance
 Just to say 'Hi,'

"Excuse me miss, may I take u out?"
She Okayed on condition if I bail her out.

I was surprised she was whoring for a living
But the gal was too hot to ignore for a thing

Just to make sure there is no misconception,
I told her I don't pay, but hers could be an exception,

700$ she set the price
I beckoned her over without thinking twice

We drove to the bank in a lightening dash,
Punched in numbers and withdrew some cash

I stuffed her bag we walked hand in hand,
Fully expecting a one night stand,

The first time I rented a hotel room
For a thirty minute bang of "Wham! bam! boom!"

But soon we were meeting every day
She was fast becoming a daily lay

The gal was a freak she got me addicted
To her magnetic pussy i was getting attached

Give the devils due, she was a perfect lay
But truth be told, I couldn't no longer pay

A freak in bed she got me saying oh! oh!
But my pockets inside out were screaming no! no!

Got to a point where i was like "WTF?"
Instead of writing a daily cheque

It might be cheaper to marry the chick
In lieu of paying for every lick,

So on a Sunday noon I walked her down the isle
With a ring to privatize her pussy in style

Five years down the marriage lane
My love for her is still insane

But when my friends say they fucked her before
I hate to admit that I married a whore.

Nobody cares!

When u remove ur thong
And condoms become a song
Nobody cares!

When u put ur legs astray
And invite Mr. x to prey
Nobody cares!

When u suck his lollipop
Without questioning his last night stop
Nobody cares!

When getting pregnant is ur fear
But diseases don't shade u a tear
Nobody cares!

When u get pregnant
And abortion becomes the cure
Nobody cares!

When u walk out the abortion room
Feeling as dirty as broom
Nobody cares!

When abortion depression brings u down
And every moment becomes a frown
Nobody cares!

When u become immune to the depression
And every pregnancy ends in abortion
Nobody cares!

When u no longer can't have kids
And u start to regret ur past
Nobody cares!

When ur Dr says ur sick
Ur in the league of the walking dead
Nobody cares!

"Fuck it!"

I dint mean to say
Your mind to decay
With these sacred word
In our transitional world
The word that people chaste
Yet love to hate
Because of it sound
When uttered around
While joking or chocking
Only to say
"Fuck it"

Did I say it again?
Am sorry to invoke
Your mind to provoke
With these ugly beauty
That makes you mad
And gets you sad
But remember it's a word
An expression of art
From an emotional heart
When one is hurt
Only to curse
"Fuck it"

I bemoan the paucity
Of adolescent literature
Filled with immorality
That they love to ape
To dance to in rap tapes
To feet-sore while humming

Oblivious of its meaning
Yet say it's just a word
That behooves ones decision
To love it or hate it
If not then
"Fuck it"

Oops!!
I have said it again
Provoking emotions
Across proportions
Am sorry to hurt
To poke your butt
But if you think am nasty
Then I beg for amnesty
But remember these is just a poem
That I use as a format
To access your mentality
To condemn immorality
So u either take it
Or leave it
If not then
"Fuck it!"

Confession

Straps! Unfastened
Bra! Retired
Nipples! Caressed
Feelings! Aroused
"Oh gosh!"

Clit! Ticking
Walls! Convulsing
Pussy! Dripping
Kitty! Begging
"Oh . . . fuck me now"

Zipper! Fumbled
Boxer! Humbled
Dick! Ranting
Pussy! Yawning
"Push it deeper"

Hips hugging
Thighs colliding
Juices splattering
Pussy! Confessing
"Best sex I have ever had

Lick u all night

Thong down
Legs wide
I wanna lick u all night

Lips parted
Fingers caressing
I wanna lick u all night

Honey coated
Kitty Ice cream laced
I wanna lick u all night

Head down
Tongue out
Am licking u all night

Tongue flicking
Clit tickling
Am licking u all night

Clit growing
Pussy glowing
Am licking u all night

Tongue diving
Warmth infusing
Am licking u all night

In and out
Nice and slow
Am licking u all night

Muscles convulsing
Pussy twitching
Am licking u all night

Nectar oozing
Juices flowing
Am licking u all night

Tremors building
Orgasms spewing
Am licking u all night

Knees locking
Toes curling
Am licking all night

Thighs shaking
Back stiffening
U Cuming with all might

Eyes closed
Mouth open
U screaming all loud

Feeling exhausted
And falling asleep
How u like me all night?

Kitty Kat

Happy like the Swaziland king
In a parade of virgin teens
It's how ecstatic and hyper I get
When I lick and kiss your kitty
The most exclusive chocolate bar
Or let me say the sweetest dream!

It's not about how u pave
But I also love how you shave
The v letter sign ending at Ur clit
Or the Nike sign saying "just do it"
That makes my cock to spring
Thirsting from Ur kitty to drink

Your kitty oozes honey n nectar,
And I think of taking a vector
But the being a gentleman of sort
My cock aside, to my tongue I resort
For every drop I wanna taste
That's why I hate the fuss or haste

With my tongue I drive it dip
Into your honey comb spot to sip
Clinging on my hair you skip
As my tongue darts Ur clits tip
You whimper to with a lot of delight
Confirming my skills are alright!

It's about time my cock to slide
You let your petals open wide
Showing me the pinky pulp,
The beauty of what I am about to gulp
Oh my! It's so delicious and exotic
So amorous sexy and erotic

Determined to lessen the burden
Between your thighs garden
I lounge and ramble in its shade
With memories that will never fade
In out and out I push
Making u laugh and blush
U start to cry in pain
Then I know by paining ur gaining

The room gets enveloped with sexual scent
The sheets get dump from sweat
As two bodies lay parallel exhausted
And when I touch your kitty's tender petals
They're covered with the sweetest dew.
Gleaming like Canadian glacier mountains . . .
I can't imagine something sweeter
It's like having Christmas in July
Oh kitty so tight so warm so wet so sweet!

Eyee-ing

Lips kissing
Temperatures rising
Fingers caressing
Hormones uprising
Hearts racing
Muscles aching
Dick rioting
Kitty oozing
Legs intertwining
Bodies meshing
Bottoms shaking
Bed creaking
Wall thumping
Sweat dripping
Lovers moaning
Juices splattering
New day dawning
To neighbors complaining
Of lyrical rhyming.

Beauty lies in the eyes of the beer-holder

I met u at the uptown bar
Next thing u were in my back seat car
How?
Beauty lies in the eyes of the beer holder
Every glance made my dick harder
True.
Courage of seduction mastered
Numbers quickly exchanged
Damn!
My house or yours? - We tossed
In my favor the coin flipped
Deal!
Boxers kicked down the stairs
Let's begin the sinful affair
Gosh!
I can't remember if we caressed or kissed
Or went straight fucking instead
Mmm!
Dick drove straight into your entrance
No need for manual reference
Oooh !
Pussy felt tighter than a button hole
Dick guessing this is a virgin mole
Yummy!
Blood trickled down ya thighs
As u moaned to excruciating highs
Aah!ooh !
See u some other day
That's all u managed to say
Bye!
After one week I could barely walk

I visited my doctor for a talk
Inference?
The blood wasn't a sign of virginity
But an advanced STD infection
Oh no!
"Next time put some protection
On that matterphuckin erection"
He yelled

I don't give a phuck

I know u hooked but I like u
I know u committed but i like u
I wanna walk her path n feel u
I wanna know if all that talk is true
I wanna know if what u write is real
I wanna know if u can walk the talk
I wanna know if u do what u write

I know u hooked and I envy her
I wanna see what is bulging in that boxer
I wanna feel my hands on that 8 inch
I wanna embrace my mouth on it
I wanna deep-throat that wonk
I wanna jam it like Cherokee the head nurse

I wanna feel it scrap my walls
I wanna feel it cruise deep in my hallway
I wanna feel every inch of ur thrust
I wanna hear u whisper those dirty words
I wanna experience the lyrical thrill and drill
I wanna see if u can make me squirt
Or cum like a Japanese geisha whatever u call it

I know u hooked but I don't care
I just wanna know if u can kneel
Down for the midnight vigil
Unleashing ur tongue n play darts on my honey pot
I wanna feel my muscles squeezing that eloquent tongue
I wanna see ur mustache dripping with my cum.

I know u hooked but I don't care
I wanna burry my fingers into ur butt
Wriggle n writhe my small frame under
ur muscular body
Quiver and squirm to ur passionate torture
Compliment ur groans with my soft moans and screams
As we finally both cruise to orgasm

I know u hooked but I don't give a a damn
I just want a day of enticement with
ur charming romantic wizard
Be the recipient of those romantic rhymes for a day
Take me to candle lit dinners
Open the car door and usher me out
Pull me that restaurant chair
Let me be awed by that gentleman side
of you in the streets
And be wowed by the freak in u
between the sheets.
I know u hooked but . . .
. . . I just don't give a fuck!!

Dicktation

When am talking about dick,
Am not talking about some 2 inch or 3 inch
midget type of dick, the size of an elevator button.
Am talking about some king Kong, 8 inch,
base ball bat size of a dick, that when I walk
into the room, ladies sigh cos they can tell
am well hung just by the conspicuous print.
When am talking about dick am talking
about a dick that when i ram it down ur
pussy walls hitting all the right places
 it numbs ur spine driving u into comma for a minute.
When am talking dick
Am talking about a dick that bends u over
like a bow making u quiver n moan like
a Puritan possessed with the Holy Spirit
"oh gosh . . . am cuming!"
A dick whose impact is echoed in the
kitchen by glasses breaking
From the strong tremors ricocheting from
deep south up the ridged walls into the atmosphere
 A dick that when I remove my pants
it makes women go religious, opening
their mouth n eyes wide as though they are
witnessing the second
coming of the messiah,
"ohh my goodness! Good lord!
among other religious epithets.
A dick that wakes up neighbors to my name,
A dick that makes neighbors to sleep with earplugs on

When am talking about dick
Am talking about a 4 stroke type of dick.
1st stroke, u close ur eyes,
2nd stroke, u have eaten have the pillow
3rd stroke, ur head is ringing stars and the moon,
unconscious of ur surrounding and happenings
4th stroke, u squirting like a fountain spring

When am talking about dick
Am talking about a dick that makes u orgasm
Making ur thighs vibrating like cooling blades of a plane,
A dick that makes ur knees to lock n toes to
coil n curl with ecstasy like Whitney on crack.

Kitchen flavor

Sunday night by the kitchen sink
I was mixing cocktail of a martini drink
He came over n stood behind
I wasn't sure what's was in his mind
I could feel his breath around my neck
I turned around to make a check
He guided my hands his belt to unclick
Behold sprung out an eight inch dick
Before I could even mumble a word
He had my hands grabbing his sword
 Down on my knees I reached to his hips
He buckled back and brushed it on my lips
Down from the bottom I licked to the top
Just like a child in a lollipop shop
I lifted my eyes to see how he looked
His eyes were closed I knew he was hooked
I grabbed my bag took out some lotion
Applied it on his dick in a circular motion
Grabbed his balls in a gentle move
And started to stroke his dick from above
Down in the middle I heard him sigh
Out came some pre-cum dropped on his thigh
In a swift move he grabbed my hips
Lifted me up to meet his lips
He sat me up in the kitchen table
Straddled my legs on the shiny marble
With muscular hands he ripped my thong
To the background rhythm of Sexual healing song
Tit for tat he was down on one knee
 Licking my pussy in a pulsating spree
I held on tight almost uprooting his ears
The more he rammed his tongue without fear

Momentary his tongue stroked my clits tip
To his shoulders i did an acrobatic flip . . . .
He lifted me up against the fridge
His massive dick scrapping every ridge
"Fuck me harder!" i started to sing
The more he intensified his rhythmic swing
As broken eggs and beer started sipping through
 the refrigerator door.
Mixing with sweat and cum dripping hitting the floor.

Please don't stop!!!

U taking a walk in the mall
u see her seated by the wall
Stop!

Brown eyes with a luxurious chest
True definition of beauty at its best
Please don't!

U ask her what's ur name
She says am out of the dating game
Stop!

She finally warms up to ur talk
And accompanies u for a walk
Please don't!

U talk to her for a while
She eventually starts to smile
Stop!

U already know her likes
She already knows ur dislikes
Please don't!

Ur lucky number is seven
And that day happens to be seven-seven
Stop!

U go home rehearsing her name
U feel like this u must tame
Please don't!

She calls u every night
And u feel y'all getting tight
Stop!

U set her up for a date
And u ensure she stays out late
Please don't!

All roads lead to ur house
She finds it hard to refuse
Stop!

u click on a movie and sit
U inching closer by bit
Please don't!

Halfway the movie u closer
Next u know u all over each other
Stop!

She loves the way u kiss
And every kiss makes her hiss
Please don't!

Clothes are thrown by the bed post
It's time to bake and toast
Stop!

U tongue between her legs
She clings on ur ears like pegs
Please don't!

U make her cherry stream
She says now give me ur cream
Stop!

Fucking her as always been ur dream
U lounge n fill her with all ur cream
Please don't!

U sex her with a porn stars marking scheme
Orgasmic she starts to scream
"Please don't . . . . stop!!
Please don't stop!!!! Please don't stop . . . !"

Sex

Tell me if it's real
If it's one great orgasm
Or if it's too dip a chasm
Tell me if it's a religion
Or an imaginary emotion
If it be a religion
Why are we quick to lust?
And not fast?
If it be an emotion
Why the physical ecstasy
And chutzpah of its fantasy
That leads to tiring
After rigorous stirring
Why the blurs and slurs
Of mind and speech
When one tenses

Tell me if it's real
If it's an expression of love
Unique love from above
To which we are its products
Our existence to feed
This biological need
If it be so
Why distaste its taste?
Why call it fornication?
And not an intimate communication?

Tell me if it's real
If at all it's a fruit
Of spiritual conduit
Insulated in fire

With a burning desire
That lovers gallop bare back
Mauling each other's flesh
Like horses in summer storm

Tell me if it's real
If it be a reverence and spirituality
Why the many bars of its alters
The pantheon of its many meanings
Stemming from its leanings
7 or 69 name them
Should we caress or suppress it
Even when it haunts ad stunts us
With commands and demands
That we can only feel but not fulfill

Tell me if it is real
If it's a surrender of individuality
That showcases our civility.
Defiant of boundaries and time
Treasured like a dime
A magical of mystery tours
A relief rain that pours
An origami of the soul
So sweet yet so foul

Tell me if it's real,
If so
Then why
Do we sweat?
To feel sweet
Tell me
If sex is life!!

Allergic to gals

I am allergic to gals
With detonating boobs
The mind numbing double D Sets
Especially when they slap them on my face
And command me to suck them naughtily
Like an overgrown baby breastfeeding

I am allergic to gals
With overwhelming bottoms
The type that unsettles wives
The neck breaking type
That when they pass and am with ma gal
I can't even blink because I will get smacked or
Bitch slapped in a second.

Am allergic to gals with
Thunderous baobab thighs
The sizzling type
That vibrates like reeds in water
At every single step
Especially when they get out of the car carelessly leaving nothing to imagination but bare definition

Am allergic to gals who talk dirty
The freaky naughty type
Who abandon their civility while in bed,
The horse riding champions
Who be shouting "uh, big daddy,
gimmie more of that big ole
. . . faster . . . . harder big daddy
Yes am allergic to gals . . . for every action there
is an equal and opposite reaction

Garlgaliciouse

Gal gal say
gal let's play
Gal gal goes into closet
gal gets dildo
Gal gal undress
Gal gal kiss
Gal gal fondle
Gal gal caress
Gal rub gal clit
Gal lick gal clit
Gal spank gal
Gal finger girlfriend
Gal 69 gal
Gal tongue gal cherry
Gal 6 dildo gal 9
Gal 9 tit for tat gal 6
Gal gal moan
Gal gal squirt on each other's face
Gal gal lick each other's cum
Gal gal happy.

Take care

Ur an adolescent bubbling with desire
And ur mama warns buoys are fire
Take care!

She seats u on the kitchen table
And tells u pregnancy is not a fable
Take care!

"I know u have started to date
But ensure condoms are never too late"
Take care!

When those bouys start to smile
Tell them to wait for a while
Take care!

Bouys who love to flirt
Are only aiming at ur skirt
Take care!

When u give them a handshake
Ensure it doesn't go beyond ur elbow
Take care!

If they invite u to their place to visit
Remember this poem and resist
Take care!

When they tell u it's only the head
Remember that head has no shoulders
Take care!

She already knows

Every Sunday morning
U out to church for praying
She already knows

U put on ur best suit
Thinking nobody knows ur pursuit
She already knows

After church u seen with that model
Taking her to ur favorite motel
She already knows

Her friends saw u with that gal
And ur Phone was off nobody could call
She already knows

U come home late at night
Filled with unknown fright
She already knows

U head straight to the shower
Forgetting ur fone and used condoms on the drawer
She already knows

She sees the racy text message
About some uptown erotic massage
She already knows

All her questions start with so, so . .
And ur answers are met with, no' no . .
U already know

U thought u could grow stronger
Unfortunately she can't handle it any longer
U already know

She packs her bags to go
That's when u admit and say "please don't go!"
U already know

U say u will never do it again
But she knows the trust will be hard to regain
She already knows

Should I or should i not? Is the question
Leave or stay, what's the option?
She already know

She hopes she won't regret
For deciding to forgive albeit hard to forget
She already knows

He decides to stick by his gun
He never cheats in a second or spun
U already knows

Its 70 years u all have grey hair
Still happily married into a wheelchair
Y'all already knew.

Freak or sleek?

Ladies say am the coolest guy.
But some say am innocent and shy . . .
My hands under their skirts when I try
Am always blushing looking to the sky

Gals get puzzled & ask me- Why
Even in sex i seem so shy
They say: - Your hands are skilled and quick,
But your eyes are shy and meek!
Those who are amused they call me a freak
But those who are amazed they say am sleek.

Can tease can't please

In a subsidized house by the government
I lived in the upstairs apartment

Downstairs was a sexy gal
Who had given me her number to call

One day she came to chat
Seated with her legs slightly apart

I inevitably stole the chance
Into her golden thighs to glance

Her red thong was so conspicuous
Convoluting my entire conscience

Seemingly she loved the torture
Provoked by her naughty gesture

Once in our comfort zone
We delved into a sexual undertone

She asked me what was my fantasy
That could drive my conscience to ecstasy

I told her sex in a movie theatre
Would make me a delectable treat

She shyly smiled n said
"It's one place I would love to get laid"

With her statement I thought I got the read
Her sexual fantasy to lead

But little did I know this gal
She wasn't an easy fall

But the type that loves to tease
Then shudders when it comes to please

Sex is sweet

Raw rough sex
Soft tender sex
Sex is sweet by any action

Missionary sex
7 or 69 sex
Sex is sweet in any position

Sex in the garden
Sex in the kitchen
Sex is sweet in any location

Black black sex
White black sex
Sex is sweet by any complexion

Buoy gal sex
Gal gal sex
Sex is sweet by any sexual orientation

Islamic sex
Christian sex
Sex is sweet no-matter your religion

Uncircumcised sex
Circumcised sex
Sex is sweet by any initiation

Carpenter sex
Judicial sex
Sex is sweet by any profession

Intellectual's sex
Student's sex
Sex is sweet no matter your level of education

Catholic sex
Protestants sex
Sex is sweet beyond denomination

Tall dwarf sex
Dwarf dwarf sex
Sex is sweet by any height comparison

Hand job sex
Gal dildo sex
Sex is sweet by any means of gratification

Partner's sex
Threesome sex
Sex is sweet in addition or subtraction

Democratic sex
Republican sex
Sex is sweet no matter your political affiliation

Ky-jelly sex
Saliva based sex
Sex is sweet by any lubrication

Porn star sex
Armature sex
Sex is sweet by any classification

Birthday sex
Wedding sex
Sex is sweet no matter the occasion

Make up sex
Break up sex
Sex is sweet no matter the situation

Money for money sex
Honey for money sex
Sex is sweet no matter the intention

Bed breaking sex
Wall thumping sex
Sex is sweet no wander the destruction

Condom sex
Skin skin sex
Sex is sweet
But use of protection.

Am not in the mood

U home from a business trip
She immediately starts to flip
"Am not in the mood"

Before u even take off ur tie
She tells u "please don't lie"
Am not in the mood

U ask her how was her day
She retorts back and says
"Am not in the mood"

In bed she is cold as a stone
She asks u to leave her alone
"Am not in the mood"

U extend ur hand to touch
She runs to sleep on the couch
"Am not in the mood"

U remind her it's now three days
She sternly looks and says
"Am not in the mood"

She is feeling a little bit insecure
But can't ask cos she is not sure
Am not in the mood

She real wants to ask u about that big mama
But instead she resorts to drama
Am not in the mood

U try to calm her down
But all u met with is a frown
Am not in the mood

U ask her to sit and talk
But instead she starts to walk
"I am not in the mood"

The love has turned to hate
Every question turns into a debate
Am not in the mood

U agree to settle for divorce
And the statement defining the cause
"Am not in the mood!!"

Let kids be kids

In the name of fashion statement
Graffiti defying décolletage to glorify
The gal child is a mobile bill board fashionata
Enveloped in immorality screaming lyrical tees
 "a dildo a day keeps the fingers clean"
To the age compressing
"Still a virgin but I love them big"

They are defined by the confines of the mall
Riding at an altitude with attitude
Pants blazed with sexual connotations
"if am a pain in the ass, then use more lubrication"
To the inviting mantra.
"holla if u wanna get laid"
The message is oblivious of their ignorance.
A decoy of marketing cloth line labels
That bemoans the paucity of parental guidance

Befuddled by the innuendo" sexy is hot"
Public school hallways are flashed with flesh
Young buoys stand to stare and "stand"
As the wheels of sexiness revolve at a pace
Bemused by their age mates age compression
With their lingerie like tank tops see through on parade
Baring the pint sized breasts standing at noon

Gauzy fabrics lined in public
An array of visible pant lines to sample
Inviting slits to their conclusive ending to follow
Underwear in miniskirts exposed at a sneeze
Underwear as out wear billed as classic
Pedophilias wet dreams invoked

Let's join hands-commodfying and sexualizing preteens to remove
Let's join hands the Video vixen influence on preteens to remove
Let's join hands-immorality behooves us to condemn
Because!!!!
These are the day's action to take
So young
So tender
So young
So spent
Let kids be kids.

Pussydicktion

Am addicted to a fraction of her waist,
The bright pinky pulp
That races my heart at a glance
And gears my mouth to confess
"I am addicted to her pussy"

Wake me up in the middle of the night
Or to the morning chirping birds
And I will faithfully say my morning glory
"I am addicted to her pussy!"

Drown me in the deepest river
Head down from the bridge of river Thames
Drowning my voice will still echo.
"I am addicted to her pussy!"

Stop me in the traffic jam
In the middle of a presidential parade
And i will still swear by the traffic lights
"I am addicted to her pussy!"

Lock me up in Guantanamo bay
Or in some rusty laceration camp
Still to the roof tops I will shout
"I am addicted to her pussy"

Seat me in an electric chair
Or make me stand on a board of nails
To the world my confession I will still sing.
"I am addicted to her pussy

Pussy talk

When am talking about pussy
I ain't talking about some Britney n socialite
Paris type of kitty
That smiles to the paparazzi even before
the faces of their owners do

When am talking about pussy
Am talking about some self respected pussy
that conceals its womanly sweetness
n secrets in a thong or panty,
Giving me the chance n anticipation
to unwrap it like a present from a gift wrap,
Sloughing that thong of with my teeth
before the passionate tongue assault

When am talking about pussy
i ain't talking about some kindergarten pussy
that cleans itself from back to front,
Am talking about some clean waxed pussy
that I don't have to use a Google map or gps
to access the entry point.

When am talking about pussy,
I ain't talking about some lose muscled pussy
that makes me feel like a tooth pick in a
mouth of an alligator,
that I have to ask "honey am their?"
When am talking about pussy am talking
about some tight kitty
that purrs to the lyrical rhythmic strokes.
"oh Bouy u killing me, shit!! u too big"

When am talking about pussy
Am talking about a tranquilizing kitty
That calms my temperamental and rampant dick
Once it asserts it's pussy squeezing
techniques on my wonk,
A kitty that makes every man to feel
like pussy is the best
Rehabilitation center in the world,
Because every man goes in rough hard but cums
Out looking innocent, n calm.

When am talking about pussy
Am talking about a reformistic pussy,
that when i go in as a naughty freaky pussy
addict talking thuggish shit like "bitch bend over
n show me what u got"
but only to come out as preacher, groaning
all religious anecdotes like "wow! Oh my! . . . good
lord! . . . This must the best pussy I have ever had."

When am talking about pussy
I ain't talking about some virgin
thinking pussy
Am talking about a tight warm kitty
That can accommodate my eight inch
wood pecker with ease.
Without the hustle and flow of blood
gushing forth.
A kitty that that makes a man to kneel
as though he about to pray.
A kitty that makes a man dehydrated
until he drinks a gallon of water.

Sexual anthem

The heat begins with just a look;
Numbers exchanged, motel booked
Sex date set, "don't be late"
Door knob turns, "am always on time"
Hands groping, temperature rising
Buttons pop, one to four
Shirts flying, hit the floor
Underwear's torn, with passionate lust
Boobs grabbed, nipples tweaked
Hands in thong, clit flicked
Sexual inferno, spreading fast
Melt baby melt, let's make it last!

Tongue gliding to hidden zone
Wetness felt "this is it"
Legs a jar, it's time for dinner
"Satsfucktion guaranteed or your money back".
Muscles flexed, "push it deeper"
"Fuck me harder", the pledge begins
Time is irrelevant to colliding thighs
Heavens can wait for this sweet insanity
Animalistic roars hit the crescendo
"baby am cuming", the anthem fades
Melt baby melt- it's time to stop!

I love the way you lie

I gave u my world to own
But now my love u disown
u blinded me with love
When I took u for an angel from above
U started to cheat behind my back
Deleting received calls to conceal ur tracks
My best friend unbuttoned ur blouse
Right in my uptown house
How could u fuck my best friend?
Yet swear it's not ur trend?
Then u rush home to kiss my mouth
After kissing another guys south
U were a virgin I thought u the tricks
Now u riding other men's dicks
Do u expect me to take the pride?
When they tell u "I love how u ride"?
Pliz don call my phone
I don wanna hear ur voice or tone

I fucked them all

It's true I fucked them all . .
I started with the religious monks
Who preach water but drink Heineken.
First were the catholic priests
Who press their chests on the altar boys
Yet they have the audacity
to summon me into the confession box.
So I invited them for a gang bang
To have a taste of these poetic flesh
I watched them fumble their zippers
But before they could thumb my ass
I oiled my mechanical dick
And hit em hard with biblical verses
Fucking their brains out the gutter
Into an orgasm of moral reality
"Thou shall not press ur chests on small buoys"

Second in line were the pastors,
These bling bling crucifix abusers
The money minting modern day
prophets of doom.
Who dispense miracles for a dime
And promise you instant salvation
I seduced them with mobile banking
To slough their pants at a blink
I fucked them in the balcony
Of their posh palatial residence areas
Where they live while their flocks wallow in poverty
I fucked them in the cockpit of their private jets
that they bought using tithes.

I breathed theological fire and brimstones down
their systems
Wetting their religiously bankrupt minds
With an awakening indelible commandment
"Thou shall not use Gods name in vain"

My next orgy was with the empty talking politicians
Who exhibit infantile thinking
as though they have tomato sauce for brains.
I knew they don't like action but talking instead,
So i seduced them to parliament building
I plugged their mouths with my mechanical dick
Just to prevent them from running their mouths
I deep throated them with tangible policies
Paraded their asses naked in parliament chambers.
Assaulted their bottoms with constitutional clauses.
Tormented them with intellectual whips of common sense.
Then finally i tattooed their foreheads with my mechanical dick.
"Though shall not give empty promises to the electorate
 that expires faster than unrefrigerated milk"

Next were the self-glorified Islamic extremists
Who kill in the name of holly war
I can get kinky sometimes.
So I pried their butts on the Rocky Mountains in the dessert.
Shoved cans of explosives in their asses to the brim.
I pounded them hard on the boulders
Did them up high on electrical poles
Flying them fast while watching the time bomb clock
I did them in the dusty building debris
I did them in irananian uranium tanks
then rolled them down the mountains in a blaze.
Detonating in their asses they all confessed
"Thou shall not kill the innocent in the name of religion"

I saved my lust for the last
The polluted worldwide media
That airs celebrity garbage for news
First was daily nation (daily nothing)

Followed by NTV (nothing to view)
Before the grand finale with celebrity news network (CNN)
I fucked them at the speed of a sewing machine
Pounded them hard like sticky keys of a keyboard
Then graphically sprayed my jeez on their satellite dishes
"Thou shall not comfort the afflicted to conflict the comfortable".

Poems by Dawn Blanchard Deep Rivers

Erotic Author from Indianapolis, Indiana Sensual, sexual erotic author and poet . . .
Creating a visual image through the volume of my words

Addiction

Rubbing my legs together to satisfy an urge
Friction created mind blowing elated hell
 yes I'm on the verge

You know the verge of eruption
Body shaking in my mind of seduction

As my heart beats I look around
Try to see who listening to my sound

Sounds so strong I can't hold them back
Louder, louder as I blow my stack

Damn that was good but not enough
I got to get out of here this shit is rough

My pussy is hurting, hurting real bad
Hell I need a stiff dick, one hard iron clad

To satisfy this desire that lays within
Orgasm after orgasm again and again

I have to admit what I want I want
What I need I need

The bottom line I'm addicted to dick
Indeed!!!!!!!!!

Is It Me I See

Sitting here glaring out the window
Trying to see if what I see is in my mind or is it my shadow

Shadows that follow me wherever I go
Trying to hide but it gives me my glow

The glow that shines deep inside
The glow that defines all my pride

Hell why should I run you will always be right there
My shadow my glow my deepest care

For those of you who wonder what my shadow may be
It is the deepest thought the feeling that arises my entity

Entity it is what it is, my drive
Hell I'm speaking on my treasure box that brings me alive

Alive with pleasure night after night
Thriving to survive in this sexual fight

Fight of a lifetime as a matter of speaking
My treasure box that's hot and leaking

Leaking my juices that seem to have a mind of their own
Hell you feel me we all grown

The shadow that is really not behind me
Shadow no more it's the beast my inner tranquility

Hide no more you have made your stand
My pussy pulsating feeling the power of my hand

Yes my pussy my shadow no longer hidden in my mind
My pussy strong to the end of time

Well Put Together

Grace style class describes the movements of my hips
The movements of my lips

Oh yes moving with style the way you like
Hips swaying to and fro stopping only for you to want more

Such grace as I make my way across the room
The heat rising hmm rising like flowers bloom

Class the last but not least
We all know without class hell stay in the streets

Behind closed doors I continue to move with style grace and class
Hell the slow grinding movements of my ass

The rising heat between my thighs
Demanding attention my body alive

Alive ready and willing needing to give
Give the loving that makes you want to live

Live in the moment live for the now
Slowly fucking you sweat falling from your brow

My tongue explores your every move
As we sync into this groove

The groove of me pleasing you and you pleasing me
Loving such tranquility

Yes I say with grace class and style
As you take me on an orgasmic mile

Gotta have it

If my pussy could talk what words would it say
It depends on the time depends on the day
On those days were I'm feeling calm and still
My pussy would say let's have a quick thrill
On the days when I count the minutes until it's time to go
That's the day I need to be fucked a constant flow
My pussy demands to be treated as a queen
In control yes, of her own wet dreams
Sometimes my pussy wants to be left alone
Not too long or it may decide to roam
 Alone to decide who and what to ride
A dick for the moment a dick for awhile
The dick that can fuck a continuous mile
Satisfying my pussy is not an easy flight
My pussy pleased morning noon and night.

Connections

My hands that hold my heart
So close and near
Intense the grip guarding it from fear
Your words slowly steal my heart
Releasing the grip I have
My body reacting to your touch,
Your scent the hidden passion in me
Heat rising the feelings of lust a new
The grip that once was, no longer holds
The beast inside released to explore
Seeking the one that has my mind
 As my grip is now replaced
Replaced with hope and interest for you
 An interest that runs deep in my well
Your passion allowed to enter and dwell
 A constant flow of desire
One that ignites a fire
Unable to calm the flames
Flames of a fire that burns so deep
The grip completely gone the passion on the rise
Your words that have consumed and hypnotized
Words that live in me, that flow from you
Constantly growing a continuous flame
Never to be extinguished
Only to forever burn, the flame
that connects me to you

Take N Time

As the heat between my thighs continues to rise
My breast, now stand at attention
Both reacting to this heated situation
Counting down the hours, minutes, and the seconds until
Until you take me in your bed and slowly have your way
Taking your tongue softly across my breast
Leaving me panting for more
Hands that explore to unlock my sensuous door
Tingling that travels from head to my toes
Waiting for your next move only you know
Your dick in hand slowly mounting me headed for my door
As you enter the depth of my soul
Fucking me the rhythm out of my control
Please, gripping the sheets gritting my teeth
Fighting to regain composure Strokes of perfection
Depth without limitations I scream without hesitation
As we reach our peak
Orgasm after orgasm continuous flow
The ultimate orgasm as my body blows.

Dreaming, Don't Wake Me

Wondering how and why what could it be
The constant thought of you and me
From the morning light until the sun sets across the sky
You have consumed my thoughts not a day goes by
That I don't think of you, picture you in my mind
Pictures of things I would love to do just to you
Images that haunt me as I close my eyes at night
The images bright in the night you glow like sunlight
The pictures so clear as I feel your touch
The touch of your lips, your tongue wet
Slowly as it glides from one spot to the next
Your presence crystal clear
Erasing all my fear
Panting and panting wanting to scream
How in the hell could this be a dream
Your presence so real, your touch I feel
You're caressing of my breast as I lay still
A dream this cannot be
The reality is you are here with me
As I slowly open my eyes what do I see
Is this reality or just my fantasy?

Power

Flavor that sent my body into a spin
The touch of your hand that leaves me wanting for more
What do I do as you decide to walk out the door
Body craving the touch I've come to adore

The situation has me contemplating walking away
Mind constantly asking will he ever stay
Thoughts go round and round with no place to land
Feelings for you, I hope you understand

See I wish you could feel the way that I do
Feelings that really have me feeling you
There is no time on how it can be
Me feeling you and you feeling me

A connection so strong the energy we share
Thoughts, feelings, actions the eye to eye stare

Something on the inside is reacting on the out
Passion, desire, wanting to explore body wanting to shout

Unspoken words between two souls
Words that build a bridge, too strong to destroy
A bridge of an unconditional connect, real not a toy

Stand in front of me and feel what I feel
The energy the power stronger than steel

The pull the force that has been created by two
To create together destiny a new

A force of two, uncommon to most
A force between souls with power from coast to coast

The power the energy the connect who knew
Unstoppable, force shared between two

Hungry

To touch you in places to take you there
Tasting wanting needing beware

Beware of the hungry that builds inside
The hunger I have will not subside

Lips wrapping around you, slowly they explore
Your scent leaves me wanting more

Slow then fast your body reacts
Knowing that you like it as a matter of fact

Bringing you to the point of explosion
Stopping quick slowing down the motion

Stopping only to savor the moment make it last
Not wanting you to cum to soon too fast

My hands replace my lips with a rhythm of ease
Steady movement aiming to please

My hunger is building higher than most
Riding you riding you from coast to coast

Stop, I slowly grind with a steady groove
Round and round, muscles tight my skills I prove

Prove to you that to pleasure you I can
My ultimate task pleasing my Man!!

The heat is boiling hot as hell
My body, your body needing to come as you swell

Letting go, as we climax together
You me the groove forever

Let's Play

Taking my tongue going round and round
The head of your dick momma's playground

Arching your back as the tip of my tongue
Plays with you dick, damn you are hung

You try to move and that is not allowed
Hell I am performing for the crowd

My fingers go over your body with the slightest touch
You wanting more as I have you in my clutch

Yes I am in control
Allowing you nothing as my teasing takes its toll

You grip the sheets heart beating so fast
You can't wait to taste this sexy ass

NO wait not yet, it is not time for you to get
Get between these thighs deep and strong
I know you want it fast and long

Frustrated hot coming apart at the seams
This is what I get in my wet dreams

Dreams that feel real, so real I wake up
Just to find I'm fresh out of luck

You have waited now it's time to please
Begging me begging me you on your knees

As you enter my pussy that throbs for you
Hell, now is the time to fuck me blue

Fuck me crazy fuck me now
Fuck me anyway you know how!!!

Quickie

Sometimes I awake with the desire to fuck
Living here alone leaves me no such luck

My pussy throbs as it whispers where is the dick
The dick needed stick after stick

My mind searches for answers to solve
I just want to be fucked not get involved

My toys I need you to quench this thirst
You know this is definitely not my first

Speed is slow working up to fast
Hurry up orgasm and batteries please last

Damn its over heart racing like the wind
But my pussy says not enough lets go again

Again and again I reach my peak
My body is tired I'm feeling weak

What do I do as I lay here and think
Hell my pussy is hungry I need the one eyed wink

Morning Love

The sun rises and another day begins
I collect my thoughts to plan my direction
And your voice slowly creeps in my mind whispering
Words oh so kind
Words that penetrate my mind my soul
Reaching passed hurt wounds of old
With the words that you speak
My body reacts
Pressure rising body shudders thoughts brought back
Thoughts of yesterday and the day before
Leaving me wanting you more and more
Wanting what I have not yet had
Sensations of your lips your touch good not bad
You entered my mind my battleground of words
But you seem to have left me speechless
I task unheard
Dreams of resting safe in your arms
Still peaceful avoiding all harm
Thoughts of your lips exploring my place
Words are flowing at amazing pace
Words that describe the feelings you create
Your lips bringing me to orgasm no room for debate
Debate the feelings that have erupted so fast
Deciding what will evolve will feelings last
Last through trials last through time
Or will time stand still, still as a mime

Hypnotic

As my mind races through thoughts of you
Wondering what are feelings that have entered my mind
Feelings that invade my heart, feelings that amazed from the start
See as I lay here anticipating contemplating my body stimulated
Going through what do I do, my body speaks it craves you
See the heat that overcomes the rational thoughts of me
Taking over pushing right all the way down while wrong rears its head
When I say wrong, who is to say
All I know is my body seems to have its way
Pussy on fire, that once was warm
Levels of frustration have determined my fate
Fate of needing to be touched, caressed and satisfied
My hand slowly explore my breast my hidden pleasure
Taking my mind on a journey with you seeking my treasure
See if I closed my eyes real tight, I will take you with me
To explore touching here and there, tongue going everywhere
My hand wrapped around and holding on tight
Not too tight just right
Moving up and down, slowing just enough, whispering a sound
Sound of pleasure sound of peace sound of ecstasy
As I take you on my journey of you pleasing me

Desire

The heat is rising when its cold outside
Thoughts of you deep inside
See I've waited for the one that fulfills
My every need
Just wanting to be pleased being set free
Free from frustrated lack of seduction
Going through life deduction after deduction
My sexual desires are greater than most
Constant let downs searching from coast to coast
Never giving up I need the most
Most of all your touch kiss and taste
Understand there's no time to waste
Now that I have you let's pursue what we have
See if your skills are mastered into a craft
Stripping you from head to toe
Allowing my lips to go where they may go
From beginning to end enjoying your flow
Speak to me, tell me what you like
Skills that never go away like riding a bike
Mounting you for the ride of my life
Life of ecstasy skills sharp as knife
As we both are about to cum
We realize what we share has made us one.

Let's talk

As you walked into the room, the strong presence of a man
No remnants of a boy
My thoughts drift, will you become my toy
As we converse, words of precision
I have come to my decision
To take you and entice my new toy
Games we play very adult to enjoy
I am in control as you let me explore
Our clothes slowly drop to the floor
Now to see all that you are
Body cut dick of a star
This my new toy well worth the wait
Putting my mind in a seductive state
State of mind thoughts run wild
Fucking you hard my favorite style
The talk that we started as been put on hold
My lips wrapped around, yes I am that bold
See we can talk later as for now I want you
Pleasure not business my thoughts my view
Licking and sucking your body reacts
You thought you could handle, forgetting the facts
Fact at hand that my pussy demands
And from what I see your dick responds to my pussies command
Placing your dick deep inside
You scream out I'm enjoying the ride
Ride of a lifetime pussy just right
Stroking you from darkness into the light
Now that I'm pleased we still have business to tend to
And as always my mind free body pleased ready to create a new.

Taboo

What have I done to deserve this?
Sitting here feeling your kiss
Lips wet traveling to all my sensitive spaces
Emotions run high expressed on my face
You touch me I flinch
Holding me tight in your clench
Eruptions of delight beyond my fight
Wrestling with thought of wrong and right
The feelings that you arouse and create
Will they determine my ultimate fate
Round and round my thoughts flow
Awaiting the erotic show
I take my tongue and taste all of you
Your reaction hmmm, feelings so taboo
See to go places I should not go
Wanting and needing enjoying the show
Energy high, sexual tension building
My bodies desire you I am feeling
Your dick my pussy a perfect match
You are the perfect catch
Perfect in so many ways, no wrong can I see
The way you touch me, caressing my every curve
I ask myself is this what I deserve

My breast

Full thick nipples erect
Soft sensitive I want to let
Let you touch lips wet
All my senses you I get
Aroused as you slowly lick
My body shutters, you make me tick
Tick tock the time passes
Engaging in a time your tongue lashes
Giving me pleasure after pleasure
As you explore my body my prize my treasure
My mind goes crazy as your touch releases
Emotions that were hidden now breezes
Past eruption my bodies abduction
Taken by you your look of seduction
All this reaction from the touch you give my breast
This is my ultimate test
Test of will test of control
You have captured my inner soul

Inner sanctity

Inside my walls you invade all of me
Swelling constantly as you set me free
Stroke and glide from the beginning to end
My body responds my back you bend
The dick of a master
Stroking me slow then faster
My inner walls as they consume all that you give
Stroking and stroking I continuously relive
See you hold the key to my inner most
My body my treasure you the host
Tongue of skill, exploring my all
Contemplating exhilarating for you I fall
You have reached the depth of my soul
Ultimate satisfaction obtaining your goal
 A lover you are a friend even more
Precious time spent you know I adore
I step into the light that shines around you
Allowing my heart to escape taboo

Drive

Day by day my body reacts to a desire so strong
Contemplating is this right or wrong
Manipulation of my thoughts
As they continuously stray, this battle that I bought
Battle with the intense desire
A burning this constant fire
All because my minds says no while my body says go
Taking my time I know that I should
To stop the burn only if I could
The levels rise and rise as I am losing this fight
Body in control needing you tonight
Stripping you from head to toe
My tongue explores places I go
Slowly licking and sucking your dick my toy
The ultimate pleasure tasting you my joy
My hands replace my lips as I continue to stroke
Stroking your dick the rhythm not broke
You ready to explode
I stop as it's not time
Mounting this I have to get mine
Hips gyrating pussy pulsating heat rising fast
Not stopping now as you slap this ass
More and more we give to each other
Cumming with power as we please one another

Listen

Will you listen to my heart
Beating slow then fast from the start
Will you listen to the unspoken words
Soft but strong like the flight of a bird
Will you listen to the song that plays just for us
Creating a groove, creating a rush
Will you listen to the vibrations that travel my spine
As you touch me lick me tongue divine
This I ask as you know what you do
My body reacts to all thoughts of you
From the moment I saw you my mind clicked
 Needing and wanting what I know hard as a brick
You excite me, challenge my mind as well
To the world, the joy I want to tell
Yes share, with all the happiness you bring
My treasure my heart my mind all want to sing
Sing of pleasure given by you
With every touch you capture me so taboo

Damn!!

Your dick is good but his was better
Still not enough as my pussy gets wetter
Thinking about the one that can satisfy
Giving me all strokes long I can't deny
See it's a shame when you think you can but you fail
To please a need pussy hot as hell
So I walk away frustrated again
Hell you boasted and bragged and your shit is a sin
Sin to think you can pleasure my treasure
You have not a clue, what you have cannot be measured
Walk away with your head held low
Feeling no pity as I had to create my own flow
Flow to relieve the frustration I got
You did not listen I need a lot
Apparently you did not believe what I said
And I had to find out you are no good in bed
So I will walk away and leave you with this
After that disappointment you don't even deserve a simple kiss!!

Clouds

My mind trying to wrap around this whirlwind that I'm in
Time spent with you has me floating high the clouds open
Open to see how high you can take me
Emotions run high can it really be
Be that you have captured my mind and my soul
Intrigued by your Presence, gathering my thoughts on a midnight stroll
See new this is open to explore
My hidden passion you've unlocked the door
You kiss me I feel the heat
Body aroused no easy feat
We embraced and the world disappears
I feel safe releasing my fears
I know not what I do
All I know is I enjoy time with you
As we explore my mind is open
A connection with you words unspoken
The thoughts of what you have to offer me
Unconditional love fantasy or our reality
The whirlwind that I will ride out
Anxious to know all about
The one that has captured me without a doubt!!!

Relaxing

Relaxing enjoying my time
Seldom I can be still as a mime
To let my mind be free and at ease
I am priority, the one I will please
Taking my time to breath in the air
Seeing everyday life, noticing not usually there
Taking a stroll no need to care
Loving this break something so rare
Needing the unknown can I have
Thoughts that enter as
I relax in a bath
Thoughts of pleasure
Seeking ones treasure
Wanting to do the unexpected to please
Not in a rush done with ease
Thoughts of the one who's always on the go
Just for the moment I go with the flow
Flow of your stride
Strutting your pride
Step by step the continuous glide
Amazing you are, as I am craving your touch
Well rested now needing so much Allow me to undress
Slowly I caress
Tasting such sweetness
As my tongue goes from place to place
Taking you to my heated space
I mount you slow then quick
Devouring your chocolate stick
Pressure rising as we continue to move
Yes we have created the perfect groove

Second chance

Have you ever wanted someone that was out of your reach
So damn good, lessons learned I want to teach
The touch of his hand has me going insane
Thoughts of his lips inside my brain
The things he does tantalizing titillating
Driving me crazy he is memorizing
Yes the things he does causes to have me damn near hypnotizing
Seethe dick that he possesses has it's way
Stroke after stroke lick after lick makes me stay
Deep inside I need you again and again
The fucking has just began
The head of his dick not giving it all making me wait; it's his call
Knowing I want you
The signs your clue
See I have searched high and low for the ultimate man
Yes giving me all that he can
My body craving needing you more and more
More I need not ready for you to walk out the door
Stay and listen to the sound, my heart beats for you
Just remember my treasure and you together so taboo

Still

Question:
As the time goes by
My mind drifts to a place of peace
Peace of mind constant thoughts running without cease
So little time
Little time to do the things I like to do
Exploring you and pleasing too
Giving me so much more
Pussy feeling the heat as your dick enters my door
Then the moment stops as the room returns to the still
Here I am at your will
Pressure rising wanting to feel you all the way deep inside
Does this exist or will I be denied
Will the strokes I crave
The tongue that sends me in a daze
Fucking me over and over like working a maze I ask again
Will I be denied
Or will you continue to let me ride

 Response:

Unsettled lust consumes me.
Rolling through me when I pick up you're sent on the wind.
I hunt you as my only prey
Eagerly await . . .
To turn you about in the sheets.
Heavy breathing.
I'm seething . . .
As the flame cannot be extinguished . .
We sweat immensely.
Orgasms crashing against the beating rocks of our bodies Like waves . . .

As the candles melt and die down.
I do not hesitate to sample your flesh and secret place with my tongue.
KNOW that I got us . . .
Where we need to be.
Making love wild and free.

Question-Deep Rivers
Response- John King Johnson

Poems by
Brockelle Nelson

About me

Words can do permanent damage so i picture me doing poetry as splattering
Permanent marker juice on my knuckles and hitting people with body shots (their minds, and bodies and souls) i love poetry because i have been damaged permanently but in a good way.
I now am closer to knowing what goes on inside
Other human beings minds other than my own.
Poetry . . . is that extra expressional shit and i give it thought bc it's like performing for a crowd of a million.
 I never know who may come across my poetry and i hope to make that person smile, cry, horny, or inspired.
. . to give that person . . Permanent damage.
You rang? Lol

My name is Brockelle Samone Nelson, before anything I am a child of god but after
that I am a poetess. I push pornographic content or poetry that incites response
from erotica to simple haikus. I am 18 years young reigning from Indianapolis, Indiana
and I currently attend Howard University in Washington DC as a freshmen.
I have career goals of course but my life is poetry, i wish i could major in it but i can't. I would do poetry for free in the dead of the winter on top of the empire state building with a dollar store thong on.
My only mission is for someone to walk away remembering my words.
As far as myself, I'm open to interpretation.
My poetry is a reflection of me.

Try Us and See

if u want ur car fixed,
date an auto mechanic.
Need opinions on shoes . . .
date a fashiony guy right?
but if u want to be talked dirty to . . .
u better fuck a poet or poetess

u betta fuck a poetess
2 hear somethin like dis,
cum hither,
i can make ya tongue slither.
u have turned me on n 7 ways
n im tryin my best to 1, 2, 3, 4, 5, 6 . . . . repay u.
2day i wanna make it clear
that dis girl is not lookin 4 a bootycall,
i just wanna get lost n ur existence and if hey
some extra terrestial loving goes down then i'm all with it
so mista what you tryna do
cause i'm digging u . . . .
u wanna fuck a poetess now
 don't u?

and if you wanna fuck a poet
then you might get hit
with one of these
excuse me miss
but eyeing you in that dress
or them sweat pants
having me want to plant a kiss
on your sweet full
clitoris
so tell me do you have a man

and if you are connected
with the species
like myself
can i just be your
sexual lyrical stand in
bend you over
and place my verbage
on your labia lips
fill your cookie jar
with my best alliteration thus far
so you can ccccccchhhoookkke
on your diction
when i'm going hard
with my spoken word
i kno observing
my beanie hat
and pen in my shirt pocket
got you thinking i'm a nerd
but i can spread my knowledge
on your thighs
and make your pussy have epiphanies
now here with this utensil
filled with black strong jiz
do you feel me?
u wanna fuck a poet, now don't you

want us female and male
to give it to you
so deep
till your intellect is spent and through
so if you wanna kick it with a rapper go to new york
and skate through brooklyn
wanna learn how to jerk then get a first class ticket
to California but ima tell you clearly
if you wanna have your forehead met with proses
so prophetically
then never seek a poser and always coming
seething to fuck a poet or a poetess

Spoken Words . . .

Words Spoken
-ehem. i walk out on stage in bra and panties- the audience gasps for air.
i see a couple of women roll their eyes i hear some grunts from the fellas
 -so, how yall doing tonight?- (good, good,)
-now, i just don't do spoken word, stage fright
and the pressure of expectations.
so . . . just feel me on this one-
 -the lights dim where the
Spotlight once was, and i begin . . . .

if spoken word
is what you want
words spoken
is what you will get
but not in front of group
this poet-ess
does em singular
and for most of my joints only for the male gender
you sit down in a secluded private room
and i stand before you . . . . naked
stripped of makeup
a paper
and clothes
youask where are my clothes?
and i laugh
this is my spoken word
my nipples speaking volumes to your soul
my clitoris quivering your hips
my torso doing 4 lines so fast
that you want more so . . .

are you willing to listen?
or are you just interested on my poems?
don't disappoint me by turning away
or be dissapointed
this is just my way
of flaunting my artistry
now if you concentrate
on the dip of my thighs
and the ink spill running down my calf
then you will hear
all the prolificness from me
that i can give
because this is what you asked for
spoken word
and words spoken through 2 ass cheeks
spread and bent over
for your full disclosure,
labia lips poised and position
for your applause
is what you'll get.

Thank you queens and kings. -snaps
Illuminate my bedroom-

Spin Cycle

to the unknown i don't know
but possibilities running through my mind
what if . . .
Silhouettes catapulted off walls
as our moans create shadows
2 temptin 2 vividly relive or describe.
so instead i lay sweaty, sex funky,
and replayed de images n my mind til orgasms
came randomly n frequently.
spun n spread me.
bent bodies n pressed down on cold counter top.
inhibitions slipped down de drain as ur colors
permanently pressed in2 me n our
"cycle" spun for 31 min until we were breathless,
n out of commission.

Real Life Dick Miracle

Silicone fantasies
i need a man that can
sexually
travel so deeply
that i forget to weep my appreciation

but since the circumstances
won't permit this
i lay back and fantasize
as i let this plastic dick do the rest

buried in my chest
impaling my core with this length
but oh, the strength of a man's chest
heaving on top of my breasts
is the ammunition i need
as my hands
penetrating with this fix
does it best

spit slightly on the shaft
dragged across my lips
suctioned up against the shower wall
i let my hunger drip for it
as i backed up
and yearned for hands to grab me aggressively
undressing me with a stare so malicious
i forget to kiss my own nipples tip

but since i'm riding on a solo trip
sat it up upright
as i smother my pussy lips around the head
and impaled up and down and around on it
i allowed it to groove and send earth shattering faithfully
speechless
orgasms
through me

this shit had become all cool to me
it's std and emotionally attachment free
tried to escape my love for men through my poetry
but that was doing nothing more then arousing me
and my hands can simply
scratch the surface
and although i've bursted creamy secretions
all over this fixture
there is nothing like the presence of live penis
to complete this picture

so as legs cocked open in stirrups
dildo pushed inside me to the pinnacle
mind is spinning slow
as i wait for
a REAL LIFE DICK miracle

Mathematical Sex Part 2

I wanna 1 2 3
Ju Ju Beans
Jump Me
Find the square root of you
69
2 legs. 2 bodies
4 lower. 4 higher limbs
2 parts
received him in
add the times
subtract the consciences
Multiply the fun
divide the legs
2 divided by 2 equals 1 : mine
when you hitting
I shiver as you calculate my derivative
deeper than saxophone keys
inserting absolute value
through me
Tongue takes 2 to tango
Let it lay on labia
to my opening sucks up your saliva
four Mississippi five
Nose dive-JACKPOT
Curved fingers-GSPOT
Proximity
divinity. fucking me one step at a time
-algebraically
taking my mind to places
introduced to new faces
like Newton and Avogadro
scratched his back as he
carried my thigh and denoted me

stiochiometrically holding
showing me my reactions to his dick action
with mole fractions
so i canceled out my inhibitions
as we switched positions
of the numerator and denominator
wide ruled, college ruled
he plastered my legs on blackboard
pounded my logic with his experimental data
charted my land with his x and y
variables in hands: taste and touch
it was too much. Phone i clutched
(P)7-(L)5-(E)3-(A)2-(S)7-(U)8-(7)R-(E)3
um passion with a suck on the butt
i screamed fuck from his punishment
checked his work
solved me backwards
began with total descended to my partial
pressure
we inclined and decreased
he constructed equations like they were
nothin i tore at the sheets
square root of give + -oh shit! equals what?
C
No!
um hmmm
what's that?
31
No!
i'm about to cum
you're not done!
shit!
Incorrect (whip)
42! (whack)
um!
severed my spirit with his sum
i've cum
delivered the perfect mathematical equation
intellect + elation equals significant delicacy

A Love Story To Dick

see
the first thing i wanna do is just talk to u lay u on my lips
and just suck on you

open my mouth wide
and envelop not a half
but the whole of you

you surging your cum in the pit of my stomach
is far from over
if i was strong enough
and bold enough
i'd sit you on my shoulders
and let your magic wand touch the back
of my throat
down past tonsils already taken
and settle in my vocal chords

no

travel south further
and land comfortably in my heart
cause that is where i hold the obligation
to dispose of any disposition of my skills

i'll have you kissing
the tip of each of these fingernails

never tell your boys

Relive The Conquest!

shoot blanks and tanks of supplement
in my stomach
in your ear with my tongue
moving it round, bout, and out
i kno you like that shit

just take one ride on this b train
and watch u quiver
got you hallucinating
cock laid on your stomach
loins shivering

no dividends
i suck for free

that's the least i cud do
the way you loving me fuckin me

i pay homage to the drama
you unleash in yo draws
i'll even lean or twist my physique
to pay extra special care to them balls

ashamed?
not at all

i claim my infatuation to you
so damn quick
i'm just touching your nipples
and letting u suck on my fingers
as i go no hands
head bobbing fast
on this dick

trip on me--shitttttttt

i'm a grown ass woman with feelings
got thoughts of running to something else
i wanna steal em

i'm hungry
my tongue is starving and my titties are
famished
can you feed me
jerk and jack yourrock in between 42 c's
yea i've manipulated your shaft so good now
u need me

my mouth
let me touch you nigga
i'll suck your dick
it's all in the love for sex
got you spent and tired
the notion of you retiring me
was put in to check
the night i blew your mind
and proposed to your dick

Conversational Mind Orgasms

fuck me with your conversation
no i am not asking for
sex from your mind
spread words out on my body
i want to feel the spasms
of your verbage
get me hot with your knowledge
on worldly topics
and devise ways on how we
can help the civilians in haiti
a plan to assist residents in New Orleans
if another Katrina ever happens again
because after the aftermath
of chandeliers
scratched backs
and a cum stained ass
what will you do to make it last?
what words will transpire
out from your mouth
and spill form lips
and get back to yours
i kno that ya body is banging
but in 20 years
everything starts saggin
and i don't mention your dick
because that colossal part of you
will shrivel
get this
work my middle
and not my pussy
or vaginal entry
better yet my cerebral

make my nervous system
say, his conscious flow
is something serial
and although i am enjoying
the number times i've squirted
and how after every romp with you
i grasp for the inhaler
because you have me gasping
i would much rather prefer
for you to give me
conversational mind orgasms

I give you words to convey my emotions
turn around and bend me over
as you inject inside me lyrical potions,
turn me back around facing you and continue
to literally blow me away with
what you say because even though i'm rocking
on your cock
i know that after our orgasm
i can always lay beside and hear you rant on
about immigration and barrack.
mouth piece so intellectual that sometimes
my tears get chocked up in my writing hand
and i scream for you to stop
you make me shutter with the words you utter
 never imagined that i'd meet a brother
so inclined with my mind as you do,
humbly conversing with me as i see your
diction float from your mouth and in to my ears like voodoo
see what you make me do write on and flow
on
till there's no tomorrow
great talks and great fucks is all i seeth to
satisfy my every need . . .

Do It Myself

i know you heard my whisper
tremor
it found it's way out of me tonight
stretched on the cotton sheets
i let my inhibitions roll out of me
onto to peppermint pussy juice stained
fingers
ummm
if only you cud feel these
vibrations that overtook me
it was straight ill
in every imaginable way
my moans
were recordable worthy
they flowed out of me
on to paper
like this . . . .
it was 7 seconds
turned into 10 min
made u gasp w/in myself
headboard clinchin
nipple pinchin
screamin to de high heavens
mufflin n 2 de pillow
it leg stiffing
mind driftin
give me a square afterwards
drippin
squritin
hurtin
crying 1

multi and mono
head nod listen 2 rock out music to
it was the ultimate
de simple
de most passionate orgasm
i jus had.

and i intend on reliving the conquest again

Greatest Philosophical Sex

inside this bed i bring you under sheets
textbooks and chocolate all over me
the moonlight strikes across your chiseled
face and you find your tongue in the place past
my waist (waist)
if we keep this up your love will collide with
my own
(inject me with your substance)
and if we keep this up then your science and
my poetry might combine
all because
of the greatest

place my knowledge
on your dick
intellectually stimulating
my greatest fix
theoretical loving
as i envelop you
my spirit you'll clutch
and my manifestations too
hold me tight
chest to breast
suck my lips
nose in my neck
philosophical love strumming through my
mind
this is the greatest sex i ever had

im trying to do 7 things to fuck your mind
i'll explore you with my wisdom until you
become mine
like da last little chapter i'll have you wanting
more
legs wide open so
you can penetrate my door (door)
if we keep this up your love will collide with
my own
(inject me with your substance)
and
if we keep this up then your science and
my poetry might combine
all because
of the greatest

save
save part of it for me
let me have you
poised perfectly
dick erect to perfection
can we make philosophical love tonight?
right-right

in to my cerebral
break me down

Mind Fuck Me 1

now that there is visitation
opportunities
for you to sneak a peek
slide under sheets
and get next to me
is pretty relevant
what's the next move
and which one will i choose
to groove pelvises with?
i want em all
on my selfish tip
but can't force myself
to lay down with
anyone
until i've been mind fucked
until some one makes love
to my nervous system
and cerebal components
until words are directed to me
that'll make me really want it
dick . . .
it's nothing
i can get it coming or going
it's easy, accessible, and free
as long as i offer my mouth
or the treasure in between my knees
but the silicone fixture
can take sure care of these desires
i need intellectual reciprocation
please
can someone mind fuck me?

preferably a man
because i'm tired of the boys
and their games
and their obvious ways they play
to get a name
so they trick you and lick you
allude that they have it under control
that they are master lovers
they know what to do
but before i expose that untruth
i need some food that stimulates
nothing blatantly sexually related
more like conversational liberation
i'm waiting
patiently
i will not squeeze a penis head in between
my buxom c's
until i am successfully
and wonderfully
mind fucked
mind fuck me please
no baby's when you aint trying to boo me
i cud see from jump
you're only motive was to screw me
and casual sex is a casualty to you
because to become fully attracted
and fall in to me wholistically
is addicting
so i'm on a mission
not for a nut or for you to make my pussy cum
or for my female ejaculatory fluids
to run wide across my inner thigh
and down my leg groove
into your oozements as one
we can get naked
hop in the bed
as long as you literally
give me some head

open up
and give me what i really have come for
i wanna be mind fucked that's all
can you handle it
or is your dick so big
that ya thinking capacity is too small?

Meow . . . Miss Kitty

ugh . . . . my po little pussy
pulsating and thumping
straight assaulting
the cotton of my panties
i hear her agonizing moans
that scream . . . feed me feed me
like a stomach growl
i hope no one notices
my pussy groaning
i try to shush her
but she attacks my legs
forcing them to lock
and squeeze together
along with my thighs
she wants the penis . . . .
and all i've been feeding her is the pen
putting myself on constriction
and warning her
that if she wants cum squirts
she will have to calm down
and imagine herself
acting out the visionaries
that my poems presents
but she's been doin that too long
and she's grown tired of it
she's even evicted my dildo
and put a restraining order on my rabbit
so when i reach for my remote control
on my keychain
i remember her allegations
of neglect
she is punishing me for

but i just don't have the goods
to rewards her small claim
i kno the dick is the fit
that she wants to reconnect with
but what she must understand
is that i am protecting her
and she pokes her tongues
spitting slobber
 making the crotch of my pants wet
. . . lucky for me, it's raining
i try and talk with her
when we're soaking
but she continues to complain
i've done endless bribes
for finger massages
and no entrapment of panties
but she aint playing
i want my dick!
is what she keep saying
and now here
sitting writing quietly
she storms in the room
making noise like
someone jumping on a ceiling
violently
i have curious glances
that turn into
concerned stares
directed at me
so i open my legs
and unzip my jeans
and say
it aint me
it's this bitch . . . my pussy

Mind Fuck Me II

you cannot believe
the unfathomable ideas
i have trapped in between
the secret concaves of my thighs
vision
of dick pillowed
in between too puffed up pussy lips
are registering
swell them
lay your tongue on the threshold
compiled with spit
smother them
palm my breasts in the palm of your hands
and continuously
with your middle forefinger
toy with the nipple
butterfly flick the tip
as u let my juice drip off your lip
on to the areola let it sit
then inhale the all of me
as i pull back and you thus pull me into you
i'm grabbing on your head
rubbing the circumference
loving the mental connection that you do
missionary
i fully allow you do contort my shape freely
spread me
you have to 1.2.3. push past the tightness
and then collideness with the slickness
wind
and encircle your hips
yea baby

hit the interior shift
that makes me flood
your hungness with my cum
tuck your head in the curve of my shoulder
and grip two ass cheeks
with the width of your hands
my . . . hands . . . behind your back
turned over
massage the middle of me
as i throw it back
pull my hair
steer the reigns
as i react
let me detonate violently
as you piledrive in to me
turn my neck facing you
demand me to look at you
you . . . got . . . me
mind fuck me baby
is that how you like it?
yes daddy that's how i want it
is that how you want it?
ummm that's how i need it
pat my ass as u hold my stomach
while you continue to beat it
knead me in to your hands
because i want an orgasm
so faithfully speechless
my eyes look directly at you
as you have boo'ed me at the point
no flirtatious conversation
no trickery
i mouth three words
as my female ejaculatory fluids
collide with your oozements
and we blend as one
. . . . mind.fuck. me

He Has To Push

contractions spread far apart
if you account 10 minutes apiece
far
sometimes
they come at five
sweat is present
on foreheads
chest are in fact heaving
BREATHE BABY BREATHE!
She is coaching him to do so
as he holds his breath
trying to release and let go
there is no time for relaxing
he has to push
out and not suck in
he wants to travel on uncharted land
and further more discover
hidden treasures
like weak spots
cum spots
areas that makes 'she' grab the sheets
or the headboards
or her breasts and smash them together
and since on her first trial run
she succeeded
it is now his turn
to reciprocate
and now
as her mouth gets to ten
she feels life

flooding inside tunnels
and giving revitalization
to the empty well
he wants to push
like this . . . . in
inside

Boop . . . Ey Qunicy

quincy-what's happenin, i'm not here right
now but if you leave your name, number and
brief message i'll get back to you, aight,
peace. boop . . . .

ey quincy
it's been a while
since we did this talking thing
and it's not like
i want to formally introduce again
just jump back in to our freak thang
i am here
and you are here
so we can twist and turn and churn
guts
like we conversed about before
just one night about 17 times
and 18 . . . if my pussy is the bomb to you
and you got the time
i want you to suck the secrets
out of my twat
as i go burying
for some of your sweet deep accent
to jump inside of me and stay
as a memory can you tie my hands up in
your soccer net and
demonstrate the agility
you boasted of
as you take your time to make
me detonate
more then twice
before you even penetrate

my gates
look quince
if i can call you that
again
we can be friends or whatever
you wanna call us for this night
i just need to experience
that 45 degree angular dick
with the smooth caramel look
and hopefully the flavor
lets toast these cellphones
and apple juices
for my district of Colombia
coming in party
and i would want nothing more
then for you to break me in
and puncture my back
with your 212 pounds of mass
laying on top
and snaking your tongue
to suck on my neck
please
hands in panties
remembering how you used
to greet
what's happening and nipples
yearning to be sucked
is everlastingly etched in my memory
the need base grant
i am trying to claim
is your name
spelled in saliva
across my chest
and your cursive pen stroke
punctured around my nipples
mmm quincy
when you get this can you call me back at
this number
-please cum 4 me or i will cum to u or for u-

or sounding like
do u want to fuck me cause i want to fuck u
doooooooo
and then tell me what you think
about this proposition
and for the road
 listen . . . . (move the phone and let him hear the wetness)
aight q
peace

Boop . . . Q Train

Boop . . this is Quincy I'm not he . . . .
Me- Q, it's me again . . .

i would like to do something different
give you audible
from my proposition
placing the phone next to my wet twat
and start flicking
juices splattering on the phone
listen . . .
because if you plant your ear
close enough to the receiver
maybe you will hear the train making its way
down my title your train . .
the Q train
so hop on
and if you decide to
then know it's on
i am ready to relax and travel on your
locomotive
i am not trying to tie any strings
because see i just wanna feel your extra
herbs and spices
pleasure seeking
is my motive
can you settle the score
i left you a message
and now as you listen to the Second one
i want more
i think you're grabbing your member
and as i remember
in December

when we were tenderly
connected sexually
you used to stroke it for me
so one more time
please touch it at the tip
and if it feels nice
and if the breathing
from my fingers
being punctured
into my clitoris lungs
sounds nice to you
then keep going and if you occasionally
hear a soft moan
sinking down
and hitting the phone
then i'd like for you to jack the bone
and groan back for me . . . i'm waiting
my pussy perspiration
is sweating
for quincy's thick heaviness
now come get it
because i posed the challenge
and now i dare you to become unsquare
and puncture a hole
that you have dreamed
but never felt
and well . . . squish squash
it's your if you . . . welp
want it
look . . . i hope you call me back
and then i'll talk you more about
my sensual thoughts
and a possible meeting
and all of that
but right now
just listen to my pussy glistening
and my fingers
making it's own mixtape
shhhh . . . .
listen

Climax, Where Are You?

can we show each other where the climax is
at?
it is not my duty
to make you bust
but it is my inquisition
to create orgasms with my pussy
and transfer them to your dick
so i can later lick the secretions
from your slit
from the nut
so can you also manipulate
your brush and stroke
my colors
painting pictures inside of me
to relive again
and want to feel again
stretch leg in acrobatic positions
so later you can say
jokingly
baby i didn't know you were a gymnast?
so in the aftermath of your tongue bath
my thighs will be sticky
from the honey dripped and
then clip the lingering sensation
with your dick
pounding a place
you already claimed your home
and i took the for rent sign down
a week ago
so the cherry that you intend

to keep on popping is sold
we can travel
get your duffel bag
and your flight pass
and we arrive to the mecca
of climatic altitude
i'll promise that
the lasting turbulence
i will capture that moment in a kodak
so we can make it last
so therefore i hope you agree to this
Excursion
to show each other where the climax is at

69x3=Mathematical Sex

we 69'ed 3 times
me on top
he on top
and then a weird position
i was aged
he was young
and from the first time his tongue penetrated
my opening
i said OH YEA I'VE BEEN MISSING
suckered in to good girls don't do
that he showed me aint nothing wrong
with a little ass getting smacked
pulled my hair when he felt he was cumming
he tried to warn me about his load
but i was thrilled by the amount
of ejaculate running
side and down his dick it dripped
the next time i sucked every drop of it
and he aint no slacker
he was goin to town on my kitten
i was trying to run from the pleasure
he kept me in place as he was getting up in it
i thought i was doing my job
as i had him standing at attention
but he took it one knotch further
when he jammed his hand all
up in my ....shit!
when i...........damn!
and he licked the ....oh
my ....
word ....

we 69'ed 3 times
me on top he under
he on top me under
we in a weird position

He Shot Me-Deep Throat Tale

i sucked the shit
out of the tip of his clip
admired the sleek and erectile function of it
so i stuck my tongue out once
and licked the shaft
tasting for the warmth of it
he pumps his bullets in to my stomach
blow!
one shot and i squint to get acquainted
with the peep hole
rubbed it touched it
stroked it
like it was my own
first two inches
prepared to travel the toll of this totem pole
boom!
second shot shocked him
inadvertedly reversed the reverberation
of the bullet
ringing through him
had the shooter of the gun
down on his knees
as i waxed him
four more cylinders of the sex pistol
i wrestled with my saliva
and i opened my tonsils and throat
all the way up
eager to relinquish the control
back over to him
so he could bust
pow pow pow!

inhaled everything down to the trigger
4 more rounds
and now i'm done with this nigga
got em laid out
because i shot em out
released all of the beast mentality
and let it spray all inside
sitting at the bottom of the pit
once he recovered
murmured out
"damn girl you the shit"
and i cleaned the residue off the tip
as i deep throated his clip

Yes, I suck dick!

my name is Brockelle Nelson
and YES I SUCK DICK
and I no longer care how you feel about it
I slob the knob
i lick the lollipop
 i've slobbered on the cock
i tongue kiss the stick
and i no longer have a problem about
revealing it
when i get on my knees
to tend to the man meat in between my
lovers leg
i made them promise never to reveal my talent
and when the question would arise in
conversation
i would screw my face in disgust
and scream ugghh i don't do that nasty shit !
but in all reality
i was doing it wild
deep throating
lots of spit when freaky
slow and melodic when passionate
his head
popped
in
and out
my mouth
i
nibbled
on his head

and licked down his shaft
and caressed his balls
and
looked at him
and butterfly flicked
his g spot
and YES I LOVE IT
u give me a man with a thick and long dick
a room
some music
and candlelight
and i'm doing
the damn thing
give head so good
u can sign me to cock-a-fella lyrics
brain so genius
he was screaming my name in his sleep
so dedicated to his meat
i slurped and swallowed
every last drop of his cum
raped his semen from his slit
yummy in my stomach
i'm in a lifetime relationship with dick
thats why my mouth
has become a playground in sexual instances
i'm that beautiful intelligent young lady
that is free with her sexuality
so YES I SUCK DICK
how should i feel about it?
am i a slut?
a hoe?
nasty girl?
may be and may be not
but for the road
it's a wonderful thing to actually suck cock
and a tremendous task to reveal it
love it

bend on your knees.
allow him to make love to your throat
spit on it
slob on that shit
more bubbles at the knob of his stick
YES I SUCK DICk
and I'm proud of it

PU-NA-NY (caramel w a side of hellafied)

ay baby can i get some of your pussy
naw my man because this pu-na-ny
is all mines
not up for sale
i retain all ownership
although when the pillow is not enough
i might invite you to come get a hit
and this aint no silly political poem
about women's empowerment
this is just me
speaking
to you
and you allow your dick to be driven
and ridden
and sucked and fucked
you bring that same dick
to me battered and bruised
and spiritually infected
and you
you
expect
me to
let you
fuck my pu-na-ny
when you don't even know where to begin
because see you cannot approach miss kitty
with this machismo act
see,
you gots to be her friend
kneel down
and have late
night conversations

pet her
look at her
take a picture
study it
before you lick it
before you stick it
before you twist
and pound
and stroke
and nut
all in it
because
see
da-ddy
this pu-na-ny
is revolutionary
now im not gonna be cocky
and say these sugar
walls are the bomb and
im not going to pompously retort
how i taste like candy
although
my scent reaks of caramel
and a side of hellafied
jus thought i'd let you know
explore her
take your mannis
and insert them inside my innie
and finger fuck me
because contrary to belief
i like that shit
get acquainted
before i let you
before i let you
raw dog my shit
you gots to be able to
stimulate me intellectually
before i allow you to marry me
sex-ually

is your dick
is your penis
is your cock
is your pogo stick
ready for the task
is your stamina enough to last more then 15
minutes
are you in for the blast
and for the ass
and not much for the pussy
because i want you to cum
but you also have to satisfy me
know that i
am woman
black and strong like the coffee
you have to wine
and dine
and stroke and poke
and get inside the mindof my pu-na-ny
before i let you sample some of miss kitty's pussy
now when you're in the shower
or you take a leak
or maybe you
just have your dick in your hand
stroke it
preserve the juices
and the erectness
and know if you dibble and dabble
and mingle with the right people
research and sanctify
let my juices become fixtures
in front of your eyes
then maybe one night
i will be submissive
and have my labia lips
give your dick's slit some kisses
but remember
although in enough time you might get a sample of
miss kitty's reaking caramel

with a side of hellafied pussy
this is still
this is still
this is still
my
pu-na-ny

Phone Sex Hangover

there is no need to think about my past
unless it was last night
no need to sit in bed with my hand
under my chin
reminiscing about past relationships
and what we had
unless i think about last night
and the 10 digits i dialed
3-3-0-8-8-1 . . . 2, 3, 4, 5, 6
his voice spoke deep
and wanted tonight
for our phone sex session to be
exciting and
dirty

covers moved to the side
legs spread
on back but still in split formation
hands traveled down to the mecca
slick wet and gooey
tight!

grabbed dildo
licked the tip
wishing it was him
wishing for the physical presence
to exert force on top of me
instead of me having to imagine
and remember what it felt like
when i felt and i

just zoned out

gripped the shaft and inserted it slowly
teases and the teased the opening
jagged breathing
baby being called on the other phone
oh shit daddy being replied
passed the threshold
got it inside
held the base of the dildo
and pounded my brown hole

pound-oh shit!
pound-mmmmmm
take out to the tip-exhale
pound back in-ahh!
slide
stroked-fuck!
pound, pound, pound
juices splattering
squirted around the obstruction
oh, baby!, david,yes fuck me!

released and then released
i could feel my female ejaculatory fluid
squirt out of me
on the bed
on the sheet
jagged breathing
chest heaving
nipples hard from my interaction
i had with myself
 again imagining
 male
him
and on top of me
wanna have the physical presence
to feel it again

so i don't have to visualize and close
my eyes real tight
to remember how it
feels again

voice rang in
-baby
conversation flowed after
with him talking
and me squirming and playing
even after he had left
i kept exploring

and now there is no need to think
about my past
no need to think about when i
talked to my so called current boyfriend last
no need to reflect on our problems
or ask myself what's next
no because last night i had some good phone
sex

My pen is my mechanical dick (no comparison)

my pen is the only dildo i need
ball pointed, assorted color cum dripped ink
that can click on and off
and you promise me
that you can give me more then he can
your the real thing so why am i wasting
all this delectable pussy on an im-i-tation
then i asked you
can u hit my walls like he
 blasting them down ?
and you whispered yea
i whispered can you fill me to the brim
to where i can fill your love in my stomach ?
and you replied mmm hell yea give me a cha-
i then screamed can u make my paper
or napkin or
even my hand cream
and create beautiful canvas
that paint pictures of
allusions and real stories ?
and he sat there dumbfounded with his rod in
his palm
comparing it to the sleekness of my BIC
 black thick pen
and said no but i can . . .
no that is enough
but then he grabbed at my breast touching
that nerve that he thought he'd know
best that
would change my mind
about voyaging on some sexual shit with him
and i leaned over

patted his dick
and kissed his forehead
"baby your i bet your dick can do
many things for me"
but it can never fuck me like my pen does
so run and find some sista blind to the
pleasure that
this writing stick holds
but it is no comparison my pen is the only dildo,
and real dick i need

7 Minutes to sunrise:
a tryst with a celebrity

the sun aint got no sympathy for us baby
it is seven minutes till sunrise
and seven hours ago as the sunset
we made negotiations to commit
to each other's desires for one night
now seven hours later
we are faced
with the reality of our compromises
we made with our tongues and bodies
and we must face the complications
of the truth

see i wanted to do the right thing
but the wrong thing in me
forced me to force you
to be with me
as you tried to resist my advances
i pulled up my skirt
and placed your hand on the open cup in
between my legs
and made you feel
made you see how wet you had gotten me
stepped in to you as your hand stepped inside of me
and whispered if only for one night
LOVE ME

then go by your everyday existence
commit to your responsibility
and place our tryst in the backseat of your mind
but forgive your loins
only partially do that

and forget
please never you
because the image of you and I
slow close together
we were not kissing
but just breathing in to each other's mouth
and down throats
will never be forgotten
you made me feel like my body was cotton
tonight you fucked me like it'd be the last
time you see
like you would refuse to witness my
 body through a picture

tattooed your name on my ass with your
tongue
didn't even smack my derriere like you
usually do
but stroked it with hot oil
and coated it with a microchip with your
tongue
the sun set as we had sex
my back did not hit the mattress once
because of the arch your loving drove in to it
you had my legs resting on your shoulders
or on some part of you
but never hitting the ground
because if they did then we would know
it was wrong
that we'd have to stop
that the night was over and now it was
 sunrise

jammed your spoon in to the contents of me
how can i ever completely wash your scent
from my body
and allow someone to come after
what we shared
hold me baby you kept saying

don't let me go back to my world
and i held you daddy
my arms went around you
and i squeezed
no i sqouze you for dear life
so you or I wouldn't have to worry
about seven hours late

the sun is playing a trickery on me baby
one minute a dark purple
indigo filled skies with clouds and stars
the next a light pink
burnt orange red
and a brunt of our actions
negotiations developed this situation
where i don't never wanna leave
but we gotta
leave you gotta leave me
and go back to your responsibility
you have to rise and set
 yourself away from me

ONE
TWO
THREE
FOUR
FIVE
SIX
SEVEN
minutes till sunrise
damn it was good
it was . . . .

WOW Factor

Wow, little daddy, didn't think u'd put it down
like that
and down u put it
had my legs going every which a way
went inside the deepest anyone possibly can
wow, little daddy u exceeded all my expectations
see, when u talked all that talk leading up to
our encounter I doubted u
I truly did,
guess u shut me up
never knew I could release that many times
had me calling the lord's name, your name,
shit, even my own name
 and the way u licked this kitty had me wishin
I could sing
so I spit a couple of melodic verses on a
track just for u
the way ur tongue tangoed, and toyed with
my inner sactums had me wondering
where did he come from
wow
 little daddy u mos def bought that wow factor
that cant get enough hide in the bush have u
churning in your seat not returning none of
ya mam phone calls kinda loving
put that boom doom,
the santa ria, the ueva,
u put it all on me
and the colossal meat u possessed in
between ur sexy thighs still has my faucet
leaking and mind spinning
u worked my walls from the left, to the right,

up and down, back, and forth, side to side
 ur D made up a new direction inside me to
go where u explored many of times that night
 recalling how u asked me "How u like it, and
Does it feel good"
Ayy papi, got me speaking espanol and I aint
no latina chica just a sucka for ya loving
wow little daddy
u brung ya A B C and D game to me that
night
u socked it to me, brung it down on me, and
definetly wooed, and misused my poo nani
soo baby I'm sorry I underestimated
the power of ya skills
because you have those and much more
wow little daddy u put it on me
put it on me, u put it on me

Downtown (Bite and Chew)

he said he wanna come over

and experience the walls inside my mouth

make his cum cling to the inside of my cheeks

spread his semen on the inner departments of my lips

feel the back of my throat contract around his slit

until he detonates past my non existent tonsils

and in to the pit of my stomach

i've been waiting on a nigga to light my fire

and he aint got that flame

but he tryna implant his seed

this nigga wants me to suck his dick

recline on my bed

as i kneel down

and run my tongue around the undercurrent of his head

massage his balls and suction cup his nuts

til he grabs my curls

and pumps hisself up to my chin

he wants to get lost in my eroticism

and lemme have my way

make him feel like a virgin again

he wanna relive the conquest

hardened dick

erection to perfection

and allow me to give him all i got

i've been dying to suck

he's been dying to oblige me

so i invite him

and he forces himself in to my talking piece

stroke for stroke

he punctures my existence

-damn be careful what you wish for

because you jus might get it

he said he wants that oral copulation

from my membrane

and wants it repeatedly

again and again and again

i have an insatiable appetite to please

but not once did he offer to get down on his knees

so upon request i do

i bend, i grip, i spit, then bite, and chew.

Poems by
Klavon Clairmont

Biography:

Klavon Clairmont started writing poetry at the age of 16(25 years old now) whiles
pursuing his Secondary School education. His talent was never fully explored seeing
that his interest was not in the field of Arts but in Sciences. However as fate would
have it after dabbling in Sciences all the way to the Tertiary level he switched to
pursue a field in law. It wouldn't be until the age of 23 that Gaiven started to write
again at the request of several of his peers who encouraged him to pursue his
dreams in the literary field. From penning poems that run through the plains from
inspirational to eroticism, from tales of romance to tales of utter despair he has
found his niche as he immerses himself in the situation of others and writes as if he
has embodied their very spirit. In 2010 Gaiven experimented with the art of erotic
writing and quickly developed a following even though he'd never previously read
erotic fiction, as such he continued to practice his craft as he sought out books by
authors in this genre so as to develop his writing style, the result of which he has
been able to write more than a dozen short stories with a lot more on the way. As
2011 approaches Gaiven has set his goals to release his first book a collection of Erotic
short stories and poems and God willing in 2012 should publish his first novel. When

not writing Gaiven reads the works of his favourite authors J K Rowling, John Grisham,
Eric Jerome Dickey and Zane. He also spends time keeping fit by playing sports,
running and working out.

Write to me my lyrical

As his words invade my mind
I imagine his pen stroking
Stripping and stroking that thirsty
pussy of mine
Thirsty for the chance to baptise his
tongue with my drip drips
As his lips lap up every drop of juice
that streams from my hips
I await to have tattoos of passion
Lustfully litter me
From my neck to my breast
Numbing nibbles
On my nurturing nipples
My chocolate pearls whimper
As they wait to melt in your mouth
Open wide
Suckle hard
And stick that sinful tongue out

I read his words as I part my legs
My fingertips are dripping
But my pussy is still bare
Bare from the strokes of his fervent pen
Bare from a body I'd long to have bend
Bend and contort my body
Like a desire filled Plasticine
Waiting to be aligned to your sexual symmetry
Waiting for you to slay my inhibitions
with your seductive sword
Infiltrate my mind with your sensual stanzas
That stains my satin sheets
As I long to warm my reality
With this fervour fantasy

Hmm the way your alliterations
alleviate my romantic request
As your prose probe the delightful
depths of a yearning woman's mind
And a barren woman's soul
So let me offer up my bodice
As I ascend your ardent altar
Let me be your muse
As I implore new perspectives
By enticing you into new positions
Just keep writing my love
And I'll keep reading
Just keep sucking my lips, walls and clit
And I promise you
I'll suck, fuck and drain your dick
Inch by incremental inch
Bit by biting bit

Drips Drips

My pussy goes drip drip
All over your lips lips
Cum floods down your face face
I hope you savour the taste taste

Drip drip
Cumming from my hips hips
Your tongue tickles the tip tip
Of my clandestine clit clit
You nervously nibble on it
Bit by bit
But I want you to go in there and munch munch
Devour me like if I'm your lunch lunch

But before you go down south
And turn my pussy inside out
Take my breasts in your mouth by
the bunch bunch
Suck on the juice from those grapes
grapes
I swear it'll send you wild like an ape
ape
These memories are so good I think I'll rewind the tape
tape
Baby your weakness like a tooth ache
My personal chiseled cheesecake
My birthday wish when I blew out the candles
Was for me to ride your ass out like a saddle
And then when we're finished you could rock me
to sleep like a cradle
Hmm boy you're mythical just like a fable

Drip drip
I hold your ass in my hands as I unzip
Relishing the taste of your dick dick
The cum drips down all over my tits tits
I spread my legs open for the plunge plunge
My body is lifted as I lounge lounge
Out of this world as you suspend me in the pleasure
of your sexual gymnastics
My flesh is melted
My mind muddled
As my orgasm scorches the very essence of my soul
Cooled down by your refreshing cream
Shot by your lyrical and physical beam
Your words mated with my mind
Before our bodies were entwined
So I leave you with this excerpt from my tale
My sweat still dripping from the bed rails
My soul released from its sexually starved jail
My heart pulsating to the beat of your strokes
Which baby have never ever failed
To stoke the fires of my orgasmic flames.

Bring me to life

You straddle me
As my silk lingerie is all that separates
your muscular exterior
From my satisfied skin
Your warmth breath tingles my nostrils
As I breathe in your lust
With new hope

This sweet sinful pleasure
Would not be possible without your love, my love
With your chiselled cheeks
Rose curved lips
Well carved nose
Deep mystical enigmatic emerald eyes

You enlightened my eyes to a beauty
I felt was lost in romantic renaissance
pages of poetic prose
Your muscular arms lifted me from my
tumultuous tomb
And placed me on your bed of love
Where dreams of love lost in this
frigid solitude could now be levitated
Back to the land of the living
Your kiss flushed me scarlet on my
dimpled soft cheeks
As my heart stole its first beats
Beats of a life worth living
Your touch, your suckle,
Your lick, your thrust
Thrusts me into a romantic realm
Reminiscent of sensually stanza

sonnets and passionate prose
Your love penetrated my body
Like your soft, sweet words caressed my ears
Deeper, deeper than I ever had
been penetrated before
So deep than we made love
You mated with my very soul

Your sweet, sensual aroma
Coffee strong scent
Awakened my nostrils to your
very presence
I melt in your warm cocoa like body
As my bed was fed flames of delirious desire
My desire
To be loved like this
Be cuddled like this
To be romanced like the Victorian debutants
Being chased and fawned after
Oh how blessed am I
To be pursued by the vigorous veins of the youth

My pores rise at the shedding of your clothes
Your magnificent nakedness, streams my eyes
to capture every square inch
Of you
My breasts heave as if your wand levitates it
with each passing minute
My nipples harden as I swallow your hard sexual wand
Hmm I would love to continue this steamy tale but I won't
For as much as I yearn you
My sweet doting love
The resurrector of my new found will to live
This glittering gemmed ring
Signifies my new life born in sin

Roses Part One

Let me court your presence my love
Read my thoughts through the prose of my poetry
Let my lust-less, love-filled lines levitate you
from your self-imposed sheltered solace
Those walls you've buried yourself
Your feelings
Your desires in

That prison will cease to be a part of your niche
As I invite you across the courtyard with me
To a quiet bistro to sip coffee
Then let's take a stroll in the field of first crushes,
chaste kisses and fleeting romances
There I'll ordain your body with glittering gifts
That will radiate the very essence of my heart
As the eyes of the sun twinkle around your very neck
The seductive scents of the world will be blended
and mixed to your pleasure
An additional asset for you to use as you entice your many admirers
Lest you not forget your benefactor who has bestowed your bodice
which a plethora of priceless privileges

Let me make a memory with you immersed in a sapphire sea of roses
For my personal preservation
For like the pavoninus dyed oasis
You have quenched my desire to pursue your love ardently
And as the constellations correlate till infinity
So will my adoration for you expand to a celestial eternity

So let's progress from flirtatious remarks and furtive glances
And let the melody of my romance
Relinquish your regrets as it runs through your eager earlobes
And soak sweetly in your marauding mind
As your thoughts entice your limbs to embark with me on this daring delicious dance
With the steps of a man raised in the ages of the renaissance
Let me lead your heart
Your soul
Your body to its deceitfully denied deliverance.

Petals of Passion

Your nose is invaded by the invigorating vapors
Of passion-red petals
I patented to procure your participation in a pulsating night
The fragrances focused on freeing you my love of incarcerated inhibitions
And indulging me as I seductively yet sacredly
Align my stem to your red rose petals

Your vision steals away to the desirous décor
Designed to delicately deter you from
thoughts of chastity
Promiscuity
But instead have your mind, heart and soul
In sync
Resonating in harmony
To a sublime sensuality

As I watch the dim glow from the room reflect on your longing face
Dimming not my hopes
Dimming not my prayers
So long you had to await this moment
It baits my breath
As I feel the erotic eruptions evaporate off your pores
and channel through my nostrils
As they forge my fantasies and optimism with this surreal reality
That seems destined to become an eternally etched memory in the story of our love

I must confess I never thought this night would come to past
I always feared your sheltered past would breed a timid love
that would end in shameless tears

I feared it cause I never thought of myself as truly worthy to be a part of the merger
of your heart
Let alone did I think our bodies would be allowed to blend and twist our pleasures
and love in a mutual climax that would attune our senses to the very frequency of
our sexuality?
Tantalisingly teasing touches that tear terrifying fears away as each fingers tastes our
seducible skin
Kisses caressing our souls
As each peck precariously prods past our flesh planting pictures to play-back in times
of pain
Melodious moans
Muting malicious mutterings
Manifesting mischief
Cusps coupling your soul and mine
Offering it a sanctuary
Saving it from a premature solitude
Sly suckles and nibbles that nibble away at life's stress
For you in my life have made me, this lost soul truly bless
Penetrations and invasions that explore and welcome the chance for true love to be
stitched using the fabrics of our bodies, the needle from my stem and the petals
 from you my radiant red rose.

A Breath of Fresh Air

You anchored yourself in my dreams before you were near
You were a sight that soothed my eyes after
being in the depths of despair
You opened my heart again to the love that it so feared
And you dared me to cherish you in a way I never thought I could for any woman again
Your beauty was drawn from the natural reserves of this earth
The honey brown eyes that showed me the sweetness of your soul
The cutest nose that drag so sensually against my skin
As you drink in the ebony musk aroma that I give off
Your soft cheeks dimpled to perfection
A perfect complement to your radiant smile
That you use ever so often to entice me into whatever be your fancy
Encased over it are full red blooded lips
Whose curvatures are a signature
Signature of the work done on the only truly faultless face
My eyes were blessed to behold

Your curvaceous bodice steals me away
To a time when a body like yours carried with it a stigma
But baby as flawless as you are I never thought
your personality could glow the way it does
The way your smile touches a room and fills it with your joy
You don't even draw jealous looks from your pairs
It's as if by being in your very presence they
themselves are beautified
Magnified with a blaze that burns through
the imperfections of others
Oh sweetheart the way you ask for nothing
Spurns me into gaining you heart's desires
For a deity like you should never be sad
Cause it goes against your very nature

And I would be a cruel man to allow such a travesty
to be committed on my watch

Oh sweetheart the way you long to please me
When it's just pleasing for me that I have you in my life
The spark that emerged from our first conversation
Dimmed any and everything that was negative around us
T he mutual tugging of the hearts
The symmetric bonding of our souls
The ties that interlocked and enmeshed us in a passion that melted away any doubts whatsoever
We were in fact simply two halves looking to become whole
But our contours and grooves merged so intricately so pristine
One would've mirrored us to the Sistine Chapel
Instead of brushes being stroked by Michelangelo
We stroked each other with brushes of trust, love and forgiveness

So these words are not mere ink on a page
But are meant to caress your ears when read to you
Meant to dissolve your mind of all thoughts except the images generated by the erection of letters to words to sentences to stanzas
These words must fill the vacuum when I'm gone
Must close the door to anyone else
The warmth I feel in writing this
Must keep you warm in my absence
The hot tears that stream down my face
Must be etched into every word every line
For only you my love held the divinity
To resurrect my heart from its seemingly eternal frigid tomb.

The Effect of A Kiss That's Not On Your Lips

The radiant glow on my caramel-coated skin
Has nothing to do with the flattery bestowed by my many ardent admirers
But rather of the beautiful kiss I received last night
You see his kiss was so enthralling
So sensual and yet he never touched my strawberry red lips
Yet his scent melted my spine in that blissful blaze
Hmm that tantalising tongue of his
So tenacious as it tunnelled through to my treasure trove
Hmm hmm
The way he gripped my trembling thighs
As he parted my hips
With his lips
So sensual
So sweet
He tasted and he liked
Then he tasted some more
Tickling my fancies
Without the inkling
Of what he did to my liquid lust
Melting in the sweat
As he set my bed ablaze
With orgasmic flames
My God!!!!!!!!
God should clone his tongue
The way he conducted my clit
With flicks and licks
Lulling me into deep passionate moans
Eyes rolling in my head
Where my fantasies have been confined
To my nymph-like mind
But his tongue released these suppressed emotions

For so many years
I've craved a kiss like this
My hands caressing his head
As my tongue encircled my lips in delight
I forced his mouth in deeper
As he painted a portrait of my every desire
With that mystical brush
That brushed away all my inhibitions
That attuned my senses
As I struggled to sit up
Only being supported by the strings
Strung by the seductive song being played on my victimized violin
Victimized by the way he took charge
The way he never let go
Never let up
Till my ear-splitting screams
Echoed in the shrillness of the night
Till my hips were now gyrating against his soft full lips
Ooooo
The way he nibbled
The way he massaged my walls
Like a masseuse releasing all my sexual tension
With one telling kiss
Yes so that's why despite what happens today
My mind will be in perpetual reminisce
Of that romantic rendezvous
Resonating resoundingly
Rhythmically releasing regrets
Relinquishing requirements
Risking ridicule
Rising raptures

Bathroom Intimacies

The steam from the water heater rises
As the hot water falls ever so elegantly over her lily white bodice
Her mind, her body and her soul
Are intimately tuned in to her erotic frequency
As she transforms from the lonely pretty face
Into a self-satisfying nymph
With her rebellious ritualistic revelry

She slides her hands over her sensually starved skin
Invoking the chemical reactions that take place under sexually charged conditions
She revels in her natural beauty
As she licks her finger tips
Toying with her mouth, as her fingers are encompassed by her thick moist lips
She caresses her breasts slowly stimulating her nipples
Which have now gone passion-flushed pink
And have tendered so hard so ripe
Like grapes waiting to be plucked, suckled and sucked
So that the juices can moisten her walls to aid her impending penetration

Her mouth echoes her longings
In subtle yet substantial moans
Her fingers gracefully graze her inner thighs
Her long nails tickling and teasing its way to the vessel
created for love making
Her fingers now stroke their way on her red-blooded canvas
Painting the sensually scribed images in her passion polluted mind
She envisions his every muscle flexed against her delicate frame
Rubbing her skin inside and outside
Performing that mystical massage of her walls

Only few mortals are blessed with the knowledge of
The knowledge to execute and conduct that orgasmic orchestra

Hmm she moans to herself
But no matter how many brushes she uses or how many different angles she strokes her canvas from
She still lacks the thickness to fill her walls to her satisfaction
Her fingers are still too short to anchor in the depths of her desires
She simply fails to massage every crevice of her wet womb
So she gently caresses her clit
Tantalizingly teasing her Holy Grail of affection
Not giving into her body's overbearing and un-bearable urge for more
Much more
Hence she holds the summit of her expectations from stolen memories ransom
As she hopes to steal future magical moments from her buried fantasies

But she denies herself no longer
As she plunges into her soft tender wet lips
The ones that open her hips
With a studded sensual shaft
That rubs roughly against her pussy
Yet strokes away her guilt
Strokes away her stress
Strokes away on her "caressable" canvas
Till the images in her mind are blurred by the delirium
she is now slave to
Her eyes have lost all focus and control as they threaten
to slip into her head
Blinding her from her very thoughts and surroundings
Transcending her into the very realm of her cherished fantasies
As her thick shaft prods and prods
Her muscles tighten and relax
Not sure if to stop this pleasurable pain or sinful pleasure
Ahh her pussy blood-shot by the internal flames
As she climbs her passion peak
Her body limp slides into her sexual tomb
Weak from her explosive screams and contortions

Screams that echoed the pleasure which boiled over from within
Her contorted body a result of being moulded by her dirty deeds
This sweet release
This un-describable euphoria
Ohh if this precise pristine moment could propagate itself perpetually
Ohh if only a man could've fucked me so

Friend or Foe

You're my boy
But she's my close friend
But the trend
Is not to make myself her boy-friend
But all bets are off
When the tears flee her eyes because of your lack of fidelity
When her self-esteem crumbles upon invasion from an enemy
As you penetrated your mistress
Leaving her body contorted in ecstasy

I greet my friend with a protective, platonic hug
But the hunger in her eyes for more
Is veiled by the hurt etched across her eyes
By the plethora of blood vessels
That emits with it, a red eerie glow
But as I choose my words carefully
So as to stem the eruption of lava
Threatening to dissolve what's left of her scarred heart
And voiding it of the capacity to love
It's my hope
That my words can inspire her to love again
To trust again
For I know there exists
The man who appreciates the beauty of her persona
Tied intricately with the drugging allure of her paralyzing angelic aura

But now she's the one who converses with me
Casual compliments carefully constructed, calling out my inner passions
To stir and blur the ambits of fantasy, reality and fidelity
She strokes my ego
With sultry sentences

That slips past my now un-guarded flesh
As she opens the dam of irreconcilable zeal
With phrases like
"If only you had been with me
Joy would dawn upon this barren plain"
Oh her sweet whispers
Which leaves me huskily catching my breath
But time isn't catching up with us
And though our time has passed for our feelings to be known public
We could on a stormy night provide each other
With a warm comforting closure
To those never-ending torturous tsunamis that threaten your walls of fidelity
Aghhh
Why must I be best mates with your lover?
Is this world so cruel?

I politely excuse myself from her pervading presence
I gather my thoughts in another room as I ponder a realistic solution
But she is subtle no longer
Her hands surprises me as she graces my passion-toned skin
With her soft pink fingers
I bite my lip
But to no avail
I know what she wants
Matter of fact what she needs
Her seduction reeks of revenge
For which I am to play a willing accomplice
I press my hands against her
I rub them signalling my acceptance
To this invitation
Which would perpetually invade the brotherhood?
Perpetually end boyish bonds
But as they say
The heart is willing
But the flesh is week
We fill the air with moans
That deeply penetrates each other's earlobes
This mutual satisfaction

Sensually slithering through the air
The pollution objected by her gasps
My performance punctuated by her grasps
As her nails are bloodied by the imprint on my willing flesh
Her legs locking me in place
As I caress the very hub of her sexual emotions
The sweet nectar easing the entry
Of my prized package
That brings with it the sheer delight
She hopes to get out of this late night visit
Ooohhh
Her eyes
Losing their focus on its external surroundings
As it focuses on the climax of this session
Her muscles clamp me harder
As she longs for it deeper
Thicker
Till her soul is dismembered
Lost in the bliss of the moment
Her breath gone from this world
As she gasps to get it back
Her voice lost in the wind-mill of this divine experience
Her body searing
As her orgasm boils over
Peppering her with sweet jolts of pleasure

As we lay naked
She again alongside my chiselled physique
Chiselling off the last bits of our platonic petulance
Looking to the horizon
To a future surely to be entitled an affair
Instead of a love
Surely to be scorned amongst those who are privy enough to hear this telling tale
We now harbour a deep secret
That has bonded us now in a way our bodies never could
Its title reads the ultimate betrayal
This was just the prologue
Chapter one now begins............

Gone forever

I don't know why I put the tears in your eyes

But believe me it's not intended

Cause though I don't show it

The dagger doesn't go through my heart

It goes through our heart

I want to be their for you and love you like the way you want me to

But there's something that keeps holding me back

It's like I love you but I don't like you

I don't like your attitude but I'm in love with your body

I've asked the lord to save my soul from the corrupt thoughts of my mind

But I'm human in the end and I'm subject to making mistakes

What I don't like is why every single mistake I make

Is treated as the unforgivable sin

You're tearing apart the chords of love my love

Leaving it so so thin

And though a single thread is keeping us together

I can't see it

Yes I can't see why this is worth saving

You've changed plain and single

You loved the church and aspired to heavenly heights

Now you've substituted it for the music and revelry of the disco lights

Yes I'll be hypocritical if I substituted you for another over this

But I'm just saying where did the innocent white flower go

Just because I de-flowered you

It doesn't mean you have to let my sinner's life poison your pure soul

Cause I didn't want you to be like me

I hate me and because I met you

I learnt to hate me less and give all of my heart to you

But is it my fault that your defenses weren't strong enough to just let my love alone
Permeate you and not my being

You're lost in my lies and iniquities

Stealing away the time we have now before it's all over

But I'm stealing the time we have so I could cherish it forever

Cause I know to you I'm just another stone on your way unto Mr. Right

But to me you were Mrs. Right

And no one else will ever come close to that vision of perfection

That vision will never extinguish

For its eternal flame burns steadily in my heart

And though the webs that entwined our souls together may have melted

The vision of your frame cutting the air

As if the breeze escorted you across the green fields on a divine chariot

To me your lover,

Your soldier

Your protector

Your dress swaying as if the angels are playing with it

Your cocoa chocolate frame cascading deliciously against your satin white fabric

My guardian angel

Who I believed to be my own special blessing from the almighty

Has turned into my haunting nightmare

And is a reminder of what happens

When demons fall in love with angels.

Afraid of Commitment

Your beauty stops me dead in my tracks
Yet the aura of your soul
Permeates the air and settles
Ever so gently on my wretched heart
Caressing away the boundaries
I've built up for all these years
As you slowly but diligently channel a way to my soul
It isn't long before I realize that you're the one
I've been searching for my whole life
Yet why am I crying
Why am I soiling the lily white carpet with time-tainted tears
Why can't I take the next step with you
Is it because my roots are still anchored in the sorrowful soil of my ex-love, my ex-fiance
If that is the case then my roots should be willing to be fertilized by your awe-struck perfection
But I'm un-willing to let go
The nightmares of my past have traversed the plains of my sub-conscious
Through the velvet veil
Into the realm of my consciousness
They pervade my thoughts daily
Like a slow acting poison
Toying whiles torturing me simultaneously
As it seeps the last vestige of faith
Faith in a new life
With a new love
With un-conditional trust at it's core
Married with a desire to be faithful
And supplemented with longevity
Forged by sacrifice
Because you couldn't give me the fruits of a relationship

Doesn't give you the right to teeter to death my new-found romance
This metaphysical prison I've found myself
Wasn't a just sentence for the crime of leaving you
Like I said earlier the soul of my anchor is still at your port
So I pray to the Gods of that supreme architect of our lives called fate
Deliver me from this yoke and I shall sin no more.

Drink Me

Drink me in your dazzling state
Let your nose open my lips before you set the pace
Lick me to sinful sensations
Paint on my walls with your tongue and behold the revelation
Please me in a way so I could exit this mundane precipitation
Pummel my palate with pounds of pristine pleasurable pulsations

Race my blood and let it course through my veins
Beat your lust in harder let me feel all the pain
Use your longer brush to resurrect my dormant passions to life
Let your muscles massage my maddening flesh as my hips open to the light

Now toast to my death
As my body jolts and jets
Let my romance rain on your face
Rivers of love carve lines laced by fate
Juicy tasty love devoid of all hate

I hope you enjoyed my orgasm my madly in love mate
Now it's time for me to overdose on you my perfect picturesque portrait.

You are in my dreams.

How do I even begin?
The mere fact that I'm not with you
Is damnation against my body
For in my loins I have sinned

I pass by your desk
In a discreet yet devious way
For my intentions for you
Is known to no one but myself
I long to massage the despair
I sometimes catch on your face
Massage away the suit
Caress away the lace

I ache to penetrate your mind poetically
With my lust linking love lyrics
Proposing to your pent up feelings of love, romance
Denied to you by many
Deceived to you by few
Destined to you by one
Me

Oh my cappuccino coloured sweetheart
My body is yearning to interrogate yours
With the passion I've kept from other women
Reserved only for my one true love
Your body's needs need only to be whispered in your mind
For our bond is tantalizingly telepathic
Let me arouse your senses with an aphrodisiac rendition of the alphabet on your lips
The ones that lead the entrance between your hips
Your walls

Where the nerves once fancied and tickled
Send off alarms that manifest itself in the air as bawls
Bawls of love
Bawls of pleasure
Balls and beads of sweat
Drown us soak us
Like the misery tears bring with the loss of a bet

Oh my future fiancée
Let me a dark renaissance knight
Invade your beating red tomb
The one that hasn't been opened for so long
The sacred inner chambers of your soul
Let me pull back the blinds
And bare myself naked for your intricate and intimate inspection
See my hurt that I carried for so long
A slow acting poison that nearly ate away at the core of my being
Nearly turning this once romantic, full of life young man
To a spiteful, un-remorseful gunslinger
Who plays Russian roulette?
With the women who fall in my crosshairs or within my radar
Baby let us mend our broken hearts
By putting our pieces together as one
Hence forging our love at the core
The glue being trust, sacrifice and honesty

Those where the thoughts that pervaded my mind on a daily basis
But your blissful beauty broke down the barriers between my conscious and sub-conscious
Now you're eternally nestled in my mind 24/7
But my reality is succumbing to my fantasies
Blurring my actions
Betraying my mind
You're threading on my dreams my love
Now I need to sew you in my life forever
Oh what a gorgeous garment we would make?

Close your eyes and let me invade your mind

They say a mind is a terrible thing to waste
And I hope after reading this
Both you and your pussy will be savouring the taste
So close yours eyes
And in the words of Shakespeare
Prepare those promiscuous pink petals to die

Relax and open the sensual portal of your brain
Agree to this aromatically and aphrodisiac assault
And leave your body
In perpetual pristine pleasures placating penultimate pleasurable pleasing pain
Pain for what your body craves
Will be imprisoned in your mind
And cut off from your enraged erogenous zones
From your vindicated vehement veins
Viscously vilifying the emotional marriage that must take place
So that your body can taste the sinful poisons placed in your promiscuous mind
So without further ado my female victim
Let my film of lust begin

Imagine you're with a clandestine chocolate coated dick
Imagine it crucifying the crevices of your cunt
Cleverly caressing your pussy as its juices protrude its delicious delight
Pulling your other senses into this erotic entrapment
Entrapped by the additive licking of a lusciously lengthy tongue
Lining your partaking pussy with mystical mines
Eagerly awaiting an electrifying explosion
That exposes your body
Drenched in sweat
Drenched in cum blissfully baptized in the cream of your chocolate crucifixion

Envision your pussy being performed by a promiscuous percussionist
Meditate on this portrait
As this orgasmic orchestrator
Wills your walls with whistles
As he blows
Manifesting melodies that marinate
Melting and wilting your wanting walls
As he plays a sensual song
Christening your craving clit
With his fastidiously fantastic fingers
He whistles and plays your pussy like the irresistible instrument that it is
Until your moans ascend to the spheres of seductive screams
Till he hits your hub
Causing a classical crescendo
Charismatically crashing
Celestial ceilings

Now un-button your blouse
And un-buckle your bra
Wet your fingers
And run them over your nipples
But as you massage
Keep your eyes close and imagine I'm massaging you there
When your panties are wet from your "dick" tating desires
Pull off your skirt and insert your plastic protrusion precisely
Insert incessantly
Invitingly
Increasing
Intensive invasions
Till the screams break into your realistic realms
And you're shocked by the utterances of your own misguided mouth
Tease your clit
Taste your cum
Relish in the revelation of your beautifully radiant body
Relish
Release
Resist restraint
Resist tantalizing temptations
Till I cum for you
Till I can cum to satisfy you.

Let Me Be Your Lover

Could I be your silk glove?
So that I may kiss upon your face
May I be a snow-white dove?
That I inspire you with awe-struck grace
May I be your one true love?
As I seduce your soul
Mystify your mind
With meaningful mythical rhymes
Alas let me pervade your spirit like an effervescent mist
Be it me who quenches your desire like a forbidden oasis
As I resurrect your heart to an eternity of bliss

Why I Can't Make Love To You

Your serene scent precedes your eye-dropping entrance
Astutely alerting me to your divine age of innocence
As I breathe in your beauty through my nostrils
The sensual images of you enwrapped in my passion fever flesh

You seduce my mind against its better nature
Ahh you rub slowly against my strong frame
Casually caressing the surface of my skin
Whiles simultaneously massaging the doubts from my troubled conscience
As my mind floats through the gates of fantasy
Leaving my reality like a distant dream
With a tender touch that is destined to lead us down a trail
Of mutually satisfying emotions
An intense interlacing of lips, tongues and hips

But how does a man
Who aspires to the very echelons of society's rank and file
Give a debutant
A nonchalant novice
Her first taste of lust-filled love
When I know she seeks a bond
That will leave us heart-stitched
A bond that she thinks would be cemented
By tying a sexual knot with our souls

But I know in my heart of hearts
That this pleasurable penetration of her
Un-touched, un-tainted and un-blemished tissue
Would cause no out-pouring of love for her
To fill my vacant heart
With the designs of a destiny involving us

Hence I can't sacrifice my impending social standing
And simultaneously sacrifice the shedding
Of her garmented grace
For my selfish sycophant release of tension
I would not be my mother's son
If I did such a ghastly act
So as my lips linger against hers for a fraction to long
I depart her presence
With a protective parting hug
I slip her a letter littered
With the torn duality of my heart and mind
I hope this letter doesn't pollute her image of me
But more so
Purges me in the sight of her
My mother and my God

Your Weakness

Your weakness is intertwined with his strength
Your eyes shy away from his chiselled features
As your nostrils are massaged by my alluring aroma
As you gasp with ransomed breaths
Your mind performing the permutations for this handsome hand
To withhold your wild waist
As he pulsates the pores on your neck's nape
Nibbling on your nipples
As your fingers nestle in his hair
His tongue tickles south
As your hands help him there
Kisses litter the lips on your hips as he goes forth
His brush at the ready to paint exclusively, exquisitely on your cocoa brown canvas
The tantalising thrusts, quenches your torturous thirst as you drink from this orgasmic
oasis

The Signature

"Why don't you answer the phone God Dammit?"
She exclaims in anger
As the rain drops beat down her resolve
Her resolve to get over her ex-boyfriend
Who despite all the pain and horror he has put her through
Still has her wired in to his frequency
As she's curled up in bed
On another stormy night
Waiting and hoping that he answers her phone call
And to come over for a night cap
But why and what has this young woman like this
A young woman who commands so much respect from her male counterparts
A woman who's stellar academic card boasts of MBA's and Bsc's
And who's climbed the corporate ladder to the rung of the Executive
This same woman's heart is held ransom to a man
A man who's major accomplishment is driving a foreign used car
How does such a woman who's mere presence serve as an unequivocal instruction in
its own right?
Be humiliated and abused
Physically, emotionally, psychologically
It's simple
It's sad but it's simple
For what she wants him for at this God-forsaken hour
Is not his protective services
She has an exuberant security kit for that
It's because she craves his flesh
For what God failed to bestow upon him mentally who overcompensated for physically
And it's these physical gifts as she thinks they are and his excellent aptitude for using his attributes

Is what has her panties in a knot
Her mind plagued by incessant memories of his milk-chocolate skin muscled and toned at every inch
Well-endowed as he caresses her with his lips, tongue, fingers and his nine inches of sheer momentary bliss
Yes for he signed his name on her spot
With a signature that has proven to be eternally endearing thus far
Enduring the tears, feeling of hopelessness
The feeling that how could someone in one miracle of a breath makes her feel as if the soles of her feet are gliding on clouds
And in the next wretched breath snuff it out and make her hit the ground with such a force that her body reverberates
With nervousness that signals his aura
Yes the questionnaire of un-certainty when he abounds by her
Which will she get the beauty or the beast?
And don't think for one second that he was her first
And hence holds some mystical fixation on her that takes a damn good man to change her view No
He didn't penetrate the walls of her virginity
But he simply took her sexual experience around the corner
To the next level or simultaneous levels
That her body has never known nor imagined it could've gone
How she wonders
How could he cherish her flesh like a desert tumbleweed tumbling unto an oasis
And then leave words and marks that take doctors and psychologists years to repair
The signature that found the right spot on the "write" page
To be permanently etched and eternally longed for
The power of a signature written without a pen
Is a power whose effects simply has no end

What's In a Kiss

Our souls mirror the dense fumes of desire clouding our eyes
My hand glides through your hair
As my Givenchy-scent sensually caress your nostrils
Drawing your face to mine like an image in the mind of Michelangelo
My fingers graze your tender dimpled face
As your mouth parts with baited breaths

Our lips
Slip gracefully over each other
As I taste your cherry flavoured lip-gloss
Your tongue prods my mouth
As you fervently explore every crevice of my oral organ
I hold my tongue as ransom
After all you have kidnapped my heart
I release
And the Sinatra starts
Signalling our tongue—tying tango
As our taste buds revel in the delight of the craving we cannot eat
Nor swallow

Without a hint of betraying the sexual explosion
Waiting to erupt
If we give into to our physical yearnings

But my tormented body overpowers my lust-filled mind
And I answer your call for unrestrained fervour
I then grip your hips as I grind my flesh into you
Teasing, testing your resolve
Your control to forgo this adolescent foreplay
And lick the cum from the glorious victory
That we simultaneously share
Our tongues continue their dance of desire

Mutually massaging our egos
As well as these erotic emblems of love or lust
I drink in the promise of true love, trust and fidelity
As I suckle ever so gently yet gallantly on your orifice
Your eyes enhancing the truth in your heart/soul
That truth has now dawned upon me
As our tongues weave our fates together
From mere bodily spectators of each other
To intertwine lovers
And last but not least soul-mates
It's amazing how our lives can be mapped out likes this
That so much could be hidden, disguised, revealed
Relieved, elevated, released
By one simple yet impassioned kiss

Latin Lust

That Latin Language
Which levitates us from our mundane missions of musical ensemble
Coupled with dance
Drawing us to each other
Like a canvas induces as artist
The canvas longing to be portrayed and framed in the imagination of the artist
While the artist longs to expose his knowledge to the virgin map

As the rhythm releases rustic restrictions
We slide our bodies
In and out
Up and down
The lyrics
Linking our minds to our bodies needs
Our bodies playing out
The panoramic pleasures conjured in our minds
As the pitch paces and pauses
So do our actions activate and stimulate
Dormant desires to discover each other
In a way that would make nymphs flood red with embarrassment
So as we dance to the music of the dead
Our flesh is moistened by the memoirs we will make
As we live life for the first time.

If I Could Love You

Everyday on work I glance into those shallow surfaces
That echo like a beacon
The un-fathomable depths of despair
For which exists no blueprint to construct a means for escape
The lines that are slowly but surely being chiselled unto your heavenly face
As life hammers the nails to seal the coffin of your loveless marriage
You leave work with a wary smile
Your husband's body warms yours with his insatiable lust
Yet your heart is in a frigid fortress
No way to get out and dare to search for love
No way for another's heart to survive that climate
To nurture or merely conjure a loving friendship
To culminate into a possible relationship
Yes the absence of true love could subdue fiery lust
To be just that fiery lust
I try to mend the gap
And give you the missing link
With kind words and inspirational phrases
To help you get through the day
But how I wish to completely open up my heart
Not betraying its true intentions with kind-heartedness
How I crave to soothe away you bodily stress with words
Words orchestrated in such a way to shine euphoria through a day of dread
Oh to caress your bodice with finger tips
That exist for the simple act of releasing the tensions
From your subtle silk textured skin
My voice deep enough to dispel any thoughts of discomfort with your present life
Tears fill my eyes
Because of the fact that I can't stop yours from sliding and staining

Your angelic face with the pangs and pains of this life
For my love even in sadness your beauty still radiates joy to others
But I'm still heart-broken
For not being allowed a chance to mend your heart
With Sunday evenings in the park
Picnics packed with care free fun, cup-cakes, scrolls filled with love penned
By the heart of your soul-mate
In the ink of my faith flowing blood
Faith that this love is true
That this love will endure
The un-escapable arguments that may threaten to wound our bond
But don't worry darling
The love doctor will always be ready to patch things up
With understanding, compromise and selfless sacrifice
Oh my sweet office muse
I ask of you and only you to let me take your heart on an eternal journey of love
I pray to you
The grand architect of the universe
To give me the courage
To thin the mist of denial
And let my true feelings paint the sky
For you to see my future love
That you won't be just mending a bond of 2 hearts
But you'll also be giving a sanctuary for two lost souls.

If You Could See Yourself Through My Eyes

If you could see yourself through my eyes
Your heart would stop at the sight of your angelic face
Those deep pools that act as the translucent surface to your soul
Your red-blooded petals
Laced with the lethal injection of passion
Your soft cheeks
So delicate to kiss
Dimpled by God's very hand

If you could see yourself through my eyes
You would be rendered breathless at the sight of your divine frame
Oh the way your curves cascade along your faultless bodice
The way your satin lingerie hugs your figure
Like a lover in heat
Your caramel coated breasts
Supple to the touch
Pink nipples
Hardened to be suckled
Your thighs
Thick pillars of lust
Waiting to be parted
Your other lips flushed pink
With an inviting aura
Seductive smell
Lures my tongue to tickle you there
These orgasmic gateways that lead to your holy grail

Oh my darling lover if you could see you through my eyes
You'd know that I never ever meant to hurt you
I never ever meant to etch lines of despair and disappointment
On your softest of skins

If you could see my thoughts with your mind
You'd know that my intentions are pure
My love is innocent
There's no pretence
There's no under-lying malice
Just un-yielding sacrifice like Christ on the crucifix

Sweetheart if you could hear my thoughts through your ears
You'd know that those words I uttered
I did so out of fear
Out of anger
I was talking without a brain
I was thinking without a heart
My love if you could hear my heart beating through your ears
You'd know of the pulsating emotions
That threatened to engulfed me on our first meeting
You'd know I designed our destiny
Before I even knew your name
You'd then know that there is no way this love could fail
My sweetheart you would know my love for you
Is fed by perpetual kindness, trust and sacrifice
Mirrored only to when Zeus first stoked the eternal Olympic flame.

The Profile Picture

To say this picture is just beautiful is an understatement
Your adorable aura
Permeates through my monitor
And fills my room with an eruptible euphoria
For as the sun hits your hair
Cascading your curls from black to honey brown
Your brows thinned to perfection
Your face as if envisaged by that temptress of a goddess Athena
Engages my senses
On this virgin threshold
This subtle
Yet seductive synchronization
Of your perfect portrait
To my romantic resonance
Your lips carefully curved
Sensually shaped
Your eyes
Dark brown pools
One would long to swim to
In order to mate with your soul
Dimpled cheeks
I long to christen with chaste kisses
That betrays my longing
To have haste
So as to not be denied
This most delectable of tastes
Your laughter
Delights my ears
As your smile distracts my eyes
And the moment deludes my mind
In a submissive slumber
For it is your body that I hunger

For
The chance to melt your caramel frame
Those muscles marinating to be caressed
Those nails itching to eat into my flesh
As you tattoo your enthralling ecstasy on my mocha skin
With a tortured tongue
Those lungs
Longing to spell out
Your delirious delight
In the longevity of my liquid lust
Which is fuelled by the quest?
Spurred by the thirst
For that pristine
Sublime
Divine
Orgasmic oasis
That whips my mind from the reality
Of just watching your face-book profile picture
To a fathomable fantasy of what would happen
What could happen?
What may happen?
If I click "Add as Friend"

How I Love Your Finger

How I love your sweet fingers
As it brushes back my stress
As you brush back my hair on my arrival from work
Your care for the little things
The intimacy of my body
That you know to every detail
Is what makes me love you my darling

Oh how I love your sensual fingers
As you stroke my face
And hold it in your hands
Offering me a warmth and security I never knew
Your eyes locked in mine
Like a fairy tale with no end
No nightmare
Just love
You kiss me
Your lips feel so snugly as it's pressed against mine
Twisting and turning
Delighting my desires
Your tenacious tongue
Exploring every orifice
As if it knew not my mouth
After all these years
You lick, you tug
With the desire of a debutant
And not the false pride of a grand-master

Oh how I love your stimulating fingers
Each finger evokes an erogenous zone
As your fingers indulge my needs

As you shed my silk, and loosen my lace
Your fingers trail the scent of my aura
My flower ready to be picked
The sweet juices oozing out
Because of the ballad you've played on my begging bodice
Hmm
An invite these fingers
As I spread my legs
Your fingers moist with your natural lubricant
Tickling my thighs
Submerging my mind in a myriad of fantasies
So that I know not
Whether it is your fingers caressing the path to my delicious doorway
Or if it is your tongue teasing and tantalising its way to my soul
No baby
You will not be refused
Neither will those manipulative fingers
As you enter you soothe
You fingers orchestrating my gasps
With their flexibility and fluidity
They conduct this sexual symphony
You toy with my clit
You methodically maneuver to "my" spot
My arena
Where my screams may deafen you
But surely not deaden you
As they serve as an aphrodisiac for a more penetrative perusal

Oh what would I do without your mood setting fingers?
Simply
Use my own with visions of you that will not hinder

The Best I Ever Had

Your butter pecan skin
Is too sweet to be denied
A tender caress
As my tongue is overwhelmed with temptation
The temptation to telepathically trigger
Teasing tensions
That is yet to be un-earthed
In this your romantic re-birth
Hmm this is so so good
Nothing had ever tickled my taste buds like this
Oh and your audaciously adorable voice
Whispering your body's wants
As my fingers
Thread through your walls
Stitching sensual sensations
To your erotic emotional ecstasies
From your mind
Ahh my love
Your lips
Lustfully lingering over
My pleasurable penetrative organ
As your hands gently
Slowly
Caress its skin
Before I ooze
My orgasmic delight in your mouth
Slithering, silently
Soulfully down your throat
The way every inch
Of your body
Pleases mines
The way your muscles grip me

As I enter your erogenous echelons
As we mutually massaging
Our members
As we milk in the delight
With our arms enwrapped around
Each other
The bed wet from our fervent frolic
Our bodies dripping with the sweat
From our erotic exercise
Your titillating tightness
Is what lulls me to your womb
Each and every time
That fantastic friction
That heats my membranes
To the point of devastating delirium
Is un-paralleled
Un-matched
By any previous sexual conquest
I may have conquered your body
By the sheer screams of your delight
But you my dear
Have conquered my mind
And enslaved my heart
As our memories
Mesmerize me
Into making more memoirs
That I seek to marry
To this mortal life

Copyright ©2010 Gaiven Klavon Clairmont

www.ingramcontent.com/pod-product-compliance
Lightning Source LLC
Chambersburg PA
CBHW030319080526
44584CB00012B/626